Over My Shoulder

Over My Shoulder

Bob Kutner

The Pentland Press
Edinburgh – Cambridge – Durham – USA

© Bob Kutner, 2000

First published in 2000 by
The Pentland Press Ltd
1 Hutton Close
South Church
Bishop Auckland
Durham

ISBN 1–85821-793–8

Typeset in AdobeGaramond 12/15
by Carnegie Publishing
Carnegie House
Chatsworth Road
Lancaster
LA1 4SL

Printed and bound by Antony Rowe, Chippenham, Wiltshire

This humble effort is dedicated with grateful appreciation to my long suffering wife Barbara who has been a most valuable, sensitive and broad-minded collaborator.

Contents

Foreword

I am delighted to write a foreword for this book. I have known Bob Kutner for some years owing to his involvement in the Senior Studies Institute at the University of Strathclyde. I was thus pleased to learn that Bob was about to publish his life story and knew that it would be a well-written and thoughtful piece of work. I was, however, unprepared for the book's contents. I knew that for a major part of his life he had lived in the south side of Glasgow and somehow thought that his upbringing would have been happy, secure and relatively uneventful. How wrong I was!

I was amazed to read about his upbringing in pre-war Europe and about the many cultures, countries and languages with which his family had to cope. Like many other Jewish families at this time they suffered discrimination, hardship and poverty and the first part of the book charts their story as they travelled from one country to another in a vain attempt to find a secure home. Following the early death of his father, his family faced especially severe financial problems exacerbated by the increasing restrictive political climate in which they lived. In the second part of the book, Bob describes his 'escape' to England, his wartime experiences and how and why he decided to settle in Scotland.

Bob describes his life with refreshing frankness and honesty. He does not flinch from describing the brutalities which he directly witnessed, or the horrendous effect of the war on his family and friends. There is however little bitterness in his book even when he is describing the worst points of his life. There are indeed many humorous and happy episodes he recounts, especially those when in the company of women!

When Bob gave me a copy of his book, he left my office with the parting promise: "You certainly won't be bored by it." How right he was. It is an excellent read and more vividly describes the human waste and destruction of war than many academic textbooks. That Bob survived to tell the story is a mixture of determination, intelligence and hard work augmented by occasional good luck and, I suspect, his charismatic charm.

I very much hope that Bob will continue to study in the Institute for many years to come. He is a prime example of how the wisdom and maturity that comes with age can be turned into a productive activity of benefit and interest to all generations.

Lesley Hart, MA, MSc, Dip.CG
Head of Senior Studies Institute
University of Strathclyde

Book 1
Germany

Chapter 1

THERE IS ALWAYS THIS FEELING that someone is looking over my shoulder, someone to ensure that I tell the story of my family and my times conscientiously and well. It should all be reported without rosy overtones, or black depressions, or yet gentle little exaggerations, or omissions or, worst of all, the grafting in of episodes that never really occurred except in books since read, or stories since heard, or events at which I may have been just a fringe spectator. Yet, after all these years, the truth does become slightly softened at the edges and it is hard to be sure of total historical accuracy, so I shall endeavour to tell my tale and ask that it may be accepted as a reasonably faithful evocation of so many years of my life gone by. Seventy-odd to be exact. Some may think that this is pretty ancient and so, let's not waste any more time and get it written before it's too late! But let me state right now that I do not feel even slightly aged, except when in the mood to be pampered by my wife, nor do I think that I suffer from the outward signs of the decrepitude of old age. In fact, my mind and body are willing and able, but my memory will just have to strain a little to reach into the past. And that little problem I shall simply have to cope with, as indeed with my poor typing, which presents another small obstacle. No doubt I shall improve with practice.

I have been given a lot of well-meaning advice on how to put this package together. Write it in longhand or use a tape-recorder or better still, buy a computer. So, lo and behold, I have bought this genie of the modern age ... a computer! In modern parlance, "state of the art". The only problem is that when I let the genie out of his bottle, a whole new problem arises: learning how to master it.

So, at least to begin with, my wife Barbara is the answer. I will dictate and she will feed my wisdom into the computer until I too learn to use it.

With that settled, we can start this story here and now, in Mallorca, where Barbara and I are sitting on the terrace of the apartment we have owned for some years. Let your imagination soar and share with us the spectacular view from our balcony. Picture it and savour it: it is May, and the temperature is perfect. Sun and sea are radiant. Over the treetops and through the trees lies the shimmering expanse of the Bay of Palma, and in the distance I can see C'an Pastilla and Arenal, sunlit jewels across the water. The twelve o'clock ferry is sparkling its graceful way to Barcelona, and the enchantment of it all is almost beyond reality: certainly a reality one could not have envisaged in those black days of the early thirties. Then, one's childhood was being smashed by a power-crazed fanatic. The enthusiastic support showered upon Hitler by the vast majority of the German people should have been enough to warn a short-sighted and deaf world of the nightmare scenario that was to unfold to its myopic, reluctant view. I am certainly not able to paint a full historical canvas of that time. Better people than I have tried, and some have even succeeded, blessed in part at least with hindsight. My hindsight therefore concerns itself mainly with personal and family memories of that time and of the years to follow. Quite a lot of events have stayed with me with great clarity, a clarity perhaps only equalled by that view from my balcony. Particularly lucid is the day Hitler came to power, as it naturally marked a violent turning point in my family's life. I was just nine years old, yet from then and even earlier I have quite vivid recollections of the atmosphere of fear, violence and indeed terror that became an everyday part of our lives. For us it was the *Götterdämmerung*, the start of the rise and rise of Adolf Hitler. That, of course, is what this tale is mainly about, but first I must sketch in a little background.

My parents were Leo (Israel Leibush) and Mitzi (Sprynza) Kutner, née Rotenstein. At the time of my birth they lived in Chemnitz where my father, although totally lacking in almost any kind of formal education, was nevertheless successfully involved in the textile industry. Thanks to his industry in other directions, my expectant mother had carried me through most of 1923, and together we had just managed to push our way into 1924, 13 January to be exact. Neither Mother nor I, the gentleman in waiting, were overcome with the news that I was preparing to enter this sufficiently difficult world the wrong way round. There may be those who feel that I have continued thus for at least these following seventy-some years ...

Chemnitz was not only the place of my birth, but also that of my brother Horst, then nearly six, and my sister Cecilie, nearly four. I was never given the impression that my complicated arrival was greeted with cartwheels of joy by my siblings and an already burdened wider world reacted with overwhelming indifference. Times were hard, and I believe that my father's business began to suffer about then. I beg that this should in no way be attributed to me! Other factors were at play, as for instance the mountainous inflation of that time. It was said that people pushed wheelbarrows laden with paper money to buy a pound of butter and that they subsisted on horsemeat and even elephant flesh from the zoo, when lucky enough to get hold of it. Later, one of my favourite playthings was to be an enormous bundle of 100,000 Mark notes, which had somehow stayed with us through the years. Did my father perhaps hope that they would one day return to their original value? At least, they made me feel richer than I have felt at any time since.

Anyway, those times of inordinate privation in Germany shaped my parents' decision to migrate to Latvia when I was two years old. We were accompanied by my father's brother Jack and his wife Sally. Since they continued to figure largely in our lives, I must tell you a little more about them. My uncle was lanky with an elongated knobbly nose and long bony fingers. He had frizzy hair and wore glasses and was possessed of a wonderfully kind and loving disposition. I feel sure that

fervour that caused them to migrate back east to Poland some time after Hitler had come to power when most others, of course, tried to head west, to the *Goldene Medineh* of America, or England, or South America and in some fortunate cases even to Palestine. However, my grandparents clearly felt the pull of the *shtetel*, and with a helpful shove from the Nazis, they went back to join their daughter Dora and her husband Leon Friedman and their three children in Warsaw. We were in touch with all of them until the start of Hitler's war: and then they all disappeared. "They all disappeared": how almost glibly one says that now! Except for one cousin, the entire family, three generations of them, dead, wiped out in concentration camps!

From Latvia, on to Leipzig. Leipzig was the big scene of our early formative years: my brother, sister and myself. Who would have anticipated that we would only have a very few years of reasonably settled childhood ahead of us and indeed, of an ordered, loving, normal family life?

At that time, the late twenties and early thirties, my father and Uncle Victor (Wicus) together with a German called Delling, had formed some kind of commercial-travelling partnership. They sold household textiles to private homes and to businesses, with varying success. Success or not, Victor and my father seemed to have themselves quite a lot of fun on their travels. Just as well, for the great depression in Germany was continuing and things were very tough. Relaxation and amusement were rare commodities, so some occasional light relief was welcome. I have the shadow of an impression that my father was perhaps not the greatest businessman. Other memories of him are clearer: of average height, slightly portly, handsome, with a moustache and a full head of hair, he tended to be slightly impatient and remote but never lacking in affection. He had a great sense of fun, which just did not surface often enough, as *tsoores* were constant companions. Looking after family and home must indeed have been

Mother and brother John in 1928

quite a handful. Our home in Leipzig was a smallish apartment in Schmidtrühlstr. 5b, in a district called Schönefeld. Recently, Barbara and I, in the company of my cousin Manfred and his wife Mirelle, made a pilgrimage to Leipzig and it was a moving surprise to see our apartment block still standing. Dilapidated, it is true, after sixty years of Nazism and Communism, but still there! We also had the nostalgic experience of seeing the home of our maternal grandparents and we spent some time at the Jewish Community Centre where we were able to view family records. We saw synagogue memorabilia from pre-Hitler days which had been miraculously salvaged and kept hidden from the Nazis during the whole of that reign of terror and then brought again to the light of day after the war.

But I am getting ahead of events. In our apartment lived my parents and later my paternal grandparents and the three of us: Horst (he renamed himself John and who could blame him?) Cecilie (to become Celia), and yours truly, Norbert, also responding to the pet name of Bertel and now Bob, much to my relief. I still use Norbert, mainly for documents and, alas, for cheques. I sometimes think that my name was designed for the amusement of my so-called friends. Well, at least it saves them thinking up worse names ... The other permanent member of our household was our live-in maid, our *Dienstmädchen*, name of Martha.

Martha was a social syndrome of the time. Everybody had one! Very much an intimate part of the family and intimate might just be the very word. I have to whisper that I think my brother John received his initiation into the mysteries of sex from our fair Martha. I should know, since she shared my room, and his nocturnal visits did create a certain stir. I suppose this was around 1932. He was fourteen and I ... well, maybe I was too young and misunderstood the whole business. Perhaps I also misunderstood my father when, having left my room one evening for a glass of water, I saw him and impartial, generous Martha in the kitchen, *in flagrante delicto*! I think

I did! I could swear I did! Clearly, Martha was a family jewel, and she seems to have taken worthy care of the family jewels of my father and brother as well ... Would that I had been older ... Be that as it may, my father's very occasional indiscretions were to cause some friction in subsequent years in other places. This apart, he was always a wholly dedicated family man. I think of us in Leipzig as a really close and happy group, despite the antisemitism already very prevalent by then.

Presumably, one of the reasons we had chosen to live in Leipzig was that my mother's father and stepmother Betti, as well as their son and three daughters, were already living there. Grandfather Süssman Rotenstein was the owner of a very successful drapery store and his family lived with him in a solid apartment in Kreuzstrasse, near the centre of Leipzig, which was a major industrial, commercial and exhibition centre and had a very substantial Jewish population.

We still followed a sound Jewish lifestyle, instilled no doubt by my paternal grandparents. Anything but a kosher household would have been unthinkable and we were devoted, regular attenders at the synagogue. One of my best memories is the glowing feeling of my father's immense woollen tallith wrapped around me at times during the Services. His hand would be on my shoulder and I melted with the bliss of those moments. I still feel that warmth. How could I have known that I would not be able to enjoy it much longer?

My parents led an active social life and amongst others, we saw a lot of my Uncle Victor and his wife Regina. My mother's beloved sister Gina was then, and always remained, a small, loving, warm bundle of energy and family dedication, in build the opposite to my mother, but with the same face. She often pretended to seem the harassed, impatient, overworked housewife, yet her eyes were full of fun. We still use family jokes that originated with her, particularly in Yiddish. Over the years, she and my mother competed at cooking and baking at which both excelled anyway. Oh, the stuffed *helzel,* the red cabbage and the unparalleled *Streuselkuchen!* To this day Barbara follows some of their recipes which obviously had their origins in Eastern Europe, since all my forebears, including my parents, had come from Poland.

For the record: my maternal great grandfather Abraham Knopf Rotenstein was born in Tomaszow, where he also died some time during the first world war and his widow, my great grandmother Cheiza née Goldman was still alive in Lodz in 1933. My step-grandmother Betti's maiden name was Brucha Kormann, and she was born in Siedlez in Russia. Her parents' names were Meyer and Yenta and they had died in Lodz.

In this connection it is interesting to note that John, Celia and I had the doubtful honour of being Polish passport holders, because of our parents' country of birth. Victor and Gina, with their sons Joe and Manfred, were in the same position. The families were close and we spent a lot of time together.

My Aunt Sally, Uncle Jack and Mother with me, aged 5

Just about then we had acquired the pride and joy of the family: an Essex Supersix motorcar. I presume it was needed for my father's business travels, but to us children it was a veritable Taj Mahal on wheels. I suppose we were not above showing it off to the neighbourhood kids. After all, at the beginning of the thirties in Germany, not so many families had cars; certainly not many of the families in our area. The car was a great help in trying to impress the girl I was definitely going to marry one day soon ... Ruth ... I wonder whatever happened to her and indeed the whole Sprung family? It is still a painful thought that this lovely little girl, with whom I played hide-and-seek during the blossom time of our romance, may have ended her young life in the horror of the gas chambers. How I hope that instead she may now be a comfortable, seventy year old matron, living somewhere in Florida, sitting beringed and bebosomed in her yard (complete with obligatory swimming pool) and praising to her friends the virtues of her very American grandchildren.

This maudlin meandering has taken me away from our Essex Supersix and the Sunday family picnics. I remember some big woods near Leipzig which were the scene of our excursions. There were also the few but spectacular holidays on the Baltic coast near Lübeck. I still have the snapshots of the happy family, of the enormous golden beaches, and of my parents in swimming costumes, looking relaxed and lighthearted: my father, hair brushed straight back, wearing a modish swimsuit with two broad shoulder straps, hands on hip, and my mother in a quite daring creation with short frilled skirt, and there was the seemingly everlasting guaranteed sunshine.

So far, I have said little about my mother. She is clearly a central figure of this story. There will be a good deal more to say about her as we go on. At this Baltic time, she was a beautiful, feminine, comfortably proportioned woman with a great capacity for enjoyment.

As for me, my next visit to the Baltic was to be under very different circumstances.

Chapter 2

ONCE MORE I SENSE that pressure to get on with my tale. The character who looks over my shoulder is prodding me on again. I must learn to resist and take my own sweet time and I certainly have plenty of that since my recent retirement. I want the leisure and space to talk about my family, and the families and people whose lives touched ours: just to ramble through the years and the countries and to do it as I please. And if at this moment this must take us all briefly back to Poland, so be it, although I confess that my knowledge of this part of our history is at best sketchy. It is all set in an atmosphere of rabid Polish antisemitism, which would later make its own eager, massive contribution to the destruction by the Germans of most of Poland's Jewish population. This antisemitism flourishes to this day, despite the savagely reduced number of Jewish residents.

As previously mentioned, my paternal grandparents joined the Friedman family who were thriving in Warsaw. As for my maternal grandfather Süssman, he and my step-grandmother Betti had originated from Lodz. Also from Lodz were my natural grandmother Stadtlender who had died not long after Aunt Gina was born, plus the Kutners and the Dessaus. The town of Lodz is not far to the southwest of Warsaw and directly north of it is the small town of Kutno; I suspect our family name derives from there.

Several of the men on both sides of my parents' families had been compelled to serve and sometimes to die for an alien cause in the Russian army during the first world war. What atrocities the Cossacks had inflicted upon the Polish Jews in their ghettoes is well documented. Being called up to the Russian army was therefore a frightening prospect and rather than submit, many Jews resorted to self-mutilation. I know that my own father had himself ruptured, with the collaboration of a sympathetic (and money-conscious) doctor. The mind boggles! Shortly after, happily unfit for military service, he left Poland for Germany in common with many other Jewish exiles. Thence followed the migration: Chemnitz, Riga, Leipzig and so on. And that is how we found ourselves in Leipzig on the day that Hitler came to power ...

Chapter 3

THE DAY THAT HITLER CAME TO POWER ... 30 January 1933. We three had gone to school as usual. We had taken the peaceful shortcut from our flat, through the gardens and backyard of our building, past some workshops, and thence directly to the main street with its massive tramcar traffic. Carefully we negotiated the dangerous crossing and there we were, safe, at the principal entrance to the school. I remember my first day there, in 1929. In keeping with the very pleasant custom of the time, I had arrived at school with my *Zuckertüte*, an enormous, colourful cardboard cone filled with sweets and such wonderful confections of all kinds; it really did make my mouth water! Just about my height it was and I still have a snapshot to remind me, standing there, proudly clutching it in my proprietorial arm.

The shortcut was the safe way to go to school, but sometimes we three chose to go the longer way, around three sides of the block, although then we were quite likely to be set upon by gangs of teenage Nazi hooligans, shouting, "*dreckiger Jude*" and "*Juda verrecke!*" Then we were happy to have our big brother as part of the trio as protector, and over the last few months we had only sustained a few minor cuts and bruises. It is hard to explain but sometimes, though quaking with fear, we were able to talk the bullies out of their aggressive stance. They liked to show what real tolerant listeners and good guys they could be and it was such a pity we were Jews, or we might have been friends, might actually even have been members of their gang! Perhaps we should have felt grateful or even elevated.

However, on this ignominious day that marks the beginning of Hitler's rule, we chose to go to school the quiet sensible way: via the backyard, dodge the trams, through the main school entrance and safely inside. But today, there is no safe feeling. Today is different. Today, you are quite clearly set apart, and immediately you sense the change. Suddenly you are Public Enemy Number One. Even the teachers' faces have altered. Where for years they had appeared to be your friends, they are now, suddenly, hateful and superior. No longer will they have to tolerate the little Jewish swine and give them equal treatment. The new system clicked into operation immediately and fear, real mind-bending, heart-stopping fear, became the order of the day.

Chapter 4

Have you ever listened to teachers in a totalitarian state giving the benefit of their Party-inspired wisdom to the pliable minds of their child-pupils?

"God is no longer the superior power: now the Leader, the Führer, is all-powerful. Now, the Führer makes the trees to grow and the flowers to bloom and the rains to fall and the rivers to flow and the sun to shine." Yes, even nature is inspired and commanded by the Leader and the previous Divinity is relegated to a minor corner of the memory. This is the beginning of indoctrination, but to an intelligent young mind it should sound, and is, totally laughable. Yet this system was common to all autocracies and I was to experience much more of it here at school and later in Italy. I was to become highly sensitive to this system of bending young minds. Thus, pupils and teachers duly spent their time eulogising Hitler, and to us Jews in the class it was made clear that we would not be allowed to share in this wisdom. We would not be tolerated among the Aryan élite. Indeed, shortly afterwards, we were given our marching orders. No longer were we to besmirch the pure minds of our former friends and fellow-pupils. As for those teachers whose Socialist or humanitarian thinking dared to linger on, they were also dismissed soon afterwards, and would experience extreme difficulty in finding other employment. The hard-core resisters among them would eventually join the Jews, the left-wingers, the intellectual elite, the gypsies and other "anti-social" elements of the state in occupying the first concentration camps, Dachau and Oranienburg.

My brother, sister and I were sent by our parents to the Karlebach

Gymnasium, named after its founder, Herr Professor Doktor Karlebach. It was the only Jewish school in Leipzig. We settled extremely well, although it meant a long tram journey every day. They called me the absent-minded professor, because I regularly left my school-bag on the tram ... I haven't changed!

This school building too we revisited recently and there is now a plaque at the side of the main entrance which reminds those interested that, during the war, it was used as an assembly point for Jews about to be transported to Theresienstadt. The inscription is very moving and ends with the words: "Lest we forget."

For the short time remaining to us in Germany, we were reasonably happy. There was a park near the school where we were still allowed to play and where I proudly acted as Cupid's messenger for my brother on his never-ending quest for girls from the school, or anywhere else for that matter. John was a good looking boy and becoming very aware of his attraction for the opposite sex. The pursuit of the ladies would ever remain one of his prime hobbies. He was nevertheless a good student and quite the probable leader of men. Celia at that stage was somewhat plainer, but did have the advantage of getting the paternal attention that girls in the family so often enjoy. She was popular at the Karlebach and indeed did quite a bit of baby-sitting for the ruling Karlebach family. To sum up, in early 1933, John was fifteen, Celia thirteen, and I was an insignificant nine year old. My father was forty-two or three, and my mother eight years younger. For the record, they had married in 1917 and John was born in 1918. Celia followed in 1920 and as already mentioned, I was born in 1924, having given my mother a hell of a time in the process.

During February, March and April of 1933, life for the Jews became noticeably worse. Hitler's accession to power was still raw and recent and he meant to prove himself. He meant to confirm the vile fulminations in his book *Mein Kampf.* He had been asked by old

Field Marshal Hindenburg, in his dotage, to form a government. At the election in January he had certainly won a landslide number of votes, but not enough to give him the absolute majority he craved in the Reichstag.

No problem! Just a few months later, his faithful acolyte and disciple Hermann Göring (*der dicke Hermann*) arranged for the Reichstag building to be set on fire. This massive conflagration gave him the instant excuse to denounce the "World Jewish Bolshevik conspiracy" as perpetrator of this crime against the German people and against the Nazis in particular. Two culprits were appointed. One was a Bulgarian called Dimitrov, and the other was a simple-minded young Dutchman called Van der Lubbe. Dimitrov was miraculously acquitted, but poor Van der Lubbe was hanged. Of course, his alleged heinous act was a carefully staged scenario for a further, larger wave of terror. Opponents inside and outside the Reichstag were ruthlessly persecuted and eliminated with the enthusiastic help of the brown-shirted SA. Jewish shop windows were smashed, homes broken into, and occupants carried off, with or without authority. Fathers of families were taken away, often never to be heard of again. The loud, peremptory knock on the door during the night became a regular terrifying fact of life. Brutality exceeded normal imagination. I still have mental images of street beatings, of elderly Jews being forced to clean gutters with their bare hands whilst being kicked and spat upon. All this under the continued management of the SA, whose bloodthirsty, foully anti-semitic Horst Wessel Marching Song struck terror in the hearts of not only its Jewish listeners. One couplet, roughly translated, boasted that the day would come when Jewish blood would spray from their SA daggers! (*Wenn das Judenblut vom Messer spritzt.*) Surely no people could have smiled benignly and applauded the import of those words and then claimed that they did not know or approve what was going on. They stood at the side of the streets cheering the SA thugs and sang it in their hundreds of thousands! But the SA's growing power and popularity did worry Hitler. In a carefully staged *Putsch*, Röhm, the SA boss, was killed on Hitler's orders and with his personal assistance. At the same time, hundreds of their leaders were butchered during the "night of the long knives" (*Nacht der langen Messer*) and subsequently the SA came under the authority of the SS, which could only be worse.

It was about this time that the first Nazi concentration camp came into being at Oranienburg near Berlin. There is a popular misconception that those horror camps were only dreamed up late in the thirties. Certainly, mass murder and Zyclon B had not yet been invented, but more sophisticated and individual atrocities were thought out and bloodily brought to bear in those days. Picture being hung by one's tied wrists over the branch of a tree for days at a time. Or standing interminably to attention without food or drink in any kind of weather. Or being made to clean the guard's lavatories by hand. Or being kicked and whipped all around the place. This treatment was not meted out to criminals, but to the cream of Jewish intellectuals, political opponents of all shades, gypsies and all other hated minorities. However, open political opposition was fast disappearing and soon Hitler and his murderers would have a free hand to implement the evil first dreamt of in *Mein Kampf.*

The tension in Germany was clearly intolerable and most Jewish households were anxiously discussing what to do. Stay or run? If so, where? Immigration into other countries was already becoming very difficult. Doors were rapidly closing. Many German Jews decided to stay. They could not believe that the persecution was aimed at them. They had occupied leading positions in commerce, in industry and the arts and sciences and had loyally served in the German army in the first world war. They thought they had automatic, built-in protection. Instead, for their simple faith, they were to have unspeakable horrors inflicted upon them. Others, mainly East Europeans

(*Ostjuden*) who were not particularly liked by the German Jews either, showed great wisdom, like my father and my uncle, in concluding that discretion was the better part of valour.

The two Kutner families and the Dessaus held a number of family councils. The outcome was that my father and Uncle Jack, who was then living in Frankfurt-am-Main, would leave for France as soon as ever possible, I really do not know why Uncle Victor and Aunt Gina did not follow the same plan, but they were to make their escape in 1935/36, direct to Nottingham in England.

Dad and Uncle Jack left Germany in 1933 with what little money they could lay their hands on and went to Lunéville in Alsace-Lorraine, France. We followed in December of that year. France was to be but the first stage in the history of the Kutner Odyssey.

Book 2
France and Switzerland

Chapter 5

DECEMBER 1933. The train journey from Leipzig to Lunéville had been unexpectedly uneventful, except for the anticipated harassment from Nazi petty officials. We had brought with us all the luggage we could possibly pack. At that time Jews were still allowed to take their chattels with them although I believe that there were severe restrictions on currency. I an not quite sure when these regulations were introduced, but I do know that at a later stage they became punitive and people had to leave all their earthly wealth behind. Anyway, it hardly applied to us, as we had very little and my father had of course taken that, in order to get us established in France. So there we stood on Lunéville station, surrounded by modest hills of baggage which represented all we owned. Our furniture we had not been able to take with us. An emotional moment, one could say, for Mother. For us children it was an adventure for, once we had crossed the German border and reached the safe haven of France, we were really able to enjoy ourselves. But oh, the uncertainty and panic my mother must have experienced on reaching this unwelcoming foreign land. Little money, few possessions and a very clouded fearsome future. But at least, on balance, it was all much better than the escalating atrocities we were leaving behind. I do believe that was the time when Mother began to show her mettle. She had her chicks about her and was determined that no harm would befall them. She would always be needing this strength and it grew appreciably through the years. I can look back on many episodes when she had to draw on all her vigour to cope with the problems we encountered.

So, finally, Lunéville. A small, typical, French provincial town quite near the German border, in the Meurthe et Moselle province. It was easy to feel at home here. I loved it immediately. It had none of the bustle and noise of Leipzig, and none of the fear. Once out of the town centre, it was a sleepy village. Trams were the major form of transport and I honestly seem to remember that they were still horsedrawn. I don't care if I'm wrong; the distance in time lends enchantment to the view. Amid great excitement we moved into our home, which was a sprawling irregular flat in a sort of bottle-neck square on the fringe of town. This square was almost a village in itself, a white Catfish Row.

The thrill of meeting my father again after several months of separation was enormous. We were all over him, until his patience came to an end. Jewish fathers did not have unlimited time for such emotional demonstrations. Priorities were different, but he did show us our new home and his and Uncle Jack's new factory which was nearby. The men had but a few steps from home to their place of work. Well, we settled in and I for one loved every minute of the place. The milkman came daily with his horse and cart and delivered his wares from vats into which he dipped a jug overflowing with frothing milk. There was also fresh country butter, eggs and cheese and for good measure he often gave me rides on his cart and I was allowed to hold the reins. Even Celia occasionally dropped her thirteen-year-old maidenly dignity to join us and once in a while big brother John lent his manly support.

Chapter 6

I HAVE MENTIONED my father's factory, though factory was a very grandiose name for a workshop where a few girls produced a selection of women's underwear. These goods were then sold to the market stalls abounding in the province. The business was of course run by my father and Uncle Jack. The manageress was a pretty woman in her twenties, whose home was directly above the workshop, and well do I recall an occasional meaningful nudge from my father to my uncle, or vice versa, when one or the other descended from the floor above in the company of a very pink-faced manageress. I was aware of more things than I should have been, because I was occasionally allowed to play in some corner of the factory. I dare say my father and Uncle Jack drew the justification for their extra-curricular activities from the difficulties and hardships they were experiencing in setting up a business in this foreign land. And difficulties there were of course in plenty, not least a total ignorance of the French language. For us children it was not so bad, because we started back to school at about that time. Fortunately all three of us showed an instant aptitude for the language.

School itself was very different from Leipzig. I was put back into the first year because of my ignorance of all the subjects that the other children had already been studying for years, but I made up quickly for my deficiencies in the three R's, plus Geography, History and French and was soon promoted to nearer my normal class level. The school building was out of the nineteenth century; so were the teachers and the customs, which included raps on the knuckles with a cane, standing in dunce's corner or being made to hang about outside the classroom for a whole period. We all, boys included, had to wear a black smock over our day clothes. The smock had a shirred waist and cuffs and a round "Peter Pan" collar. We all must have looked delightfully feminine in our puffed-out smocks and sleeves. At assembly every morning, the entire school was made to form up on the principal stairway of the building with the smallest child in front, at the bottom of the stairs, and the tallest on top at the rear, so that we might all see and be seen. Thus positioned, we sang the Marseillaise with varying degrees of ardour and tunefulness, but always good and loud. I must be one of the few septuagenarians who can still remember the children's verse of that anthem.

Anyway, school and Lunéville proved no great obstacle, and I loved the life, but it was harder for Mother. Money was in short supply, and for an extremely fashion-conscious woman, the limitations must have been irksome. Back in Germany, she had been some smart dresser, with her felt cloche hats and fur-trimmed coats, These were much less in evidence now, as was her cheerful singing of bygone days. She really had no voice, but knew the lyrics and music of every operetta and hit-musical since the beginning of the century.

Sadly, I have no voice either (why do we always seem to inherit our parents' negative qualities, not their strengths?) but thanks to her, I too can give you chapter and verse of *Schläger*, operettas and musical comedies such as "White Horse Inn", "The Student Prince", "The Merry Widow" and the songs of matinee idol Richard Tauber and still more. Nor was my mother above singing some risqué versions of hit songs and operas and these too were added to my repertoire, although by the time Mother and I successively mangled the tunes, they were quite unrecognisable. But all that was for her lighter moments. and these were becoming much less frequent. We were now in 1934; she was thirty-six and the good life had really begun to desert her. For her, Lunéville must have been a dreadful backwater, so that Paris, when it beckoned, surely appeared like a mirage ...

Later, when Barbara and I were married, she became acquainted with many operatic arias from the way I sang them. When eventually we did get to the opera together she was astonished that the performers seemed to have the tunes all wrong!

Chapter 7

THE BUSINESS had not been working out very well and plans were quickly formed to restart in Paris. But here, my parents had made their reckoning without the host. Business licences and work permits were practically impossible to obtain, except with great amounts of money to grease the grasping, greedy, avaricious claws of the petty French officials. To have to experience corruption and antisemitism as practised by the French Administration of that time was deeply disappointing and anti-climactic. Day after day I watched my poor father going out to do battle with officialdom, in an effort to secure permission to earn sustenance for his family. It was tilting at windmills! I saw him come home daily, looking defeated and demoralised. Here he was, aged about forty-four, supposedly at the peak of his life, yet unable to provide for his family, even to the lowest standard. No job, no business. No hope of getting either and suspicions were developing that his health was not as it should be. This marked the time when our fortunes sank to their lowest level. Near-starvation and privation were constant companions.

Poverty is not just an ugly word. It is an ugly fact. Our funds gone, our possessions long since hocked, my father mainly unemployed and legally unemployable, we three children too young to help ... where next? We were not alone in our misery. Many other Jewish refugee families were in equal shape and with some of them we shared living space in an alleged hotel, cynically called Hôtel de l'Ésperance. in the eponymous Rue de l'Ésperance, in the even then notoriously slummy 13th Arrondissement. It was a wretched place, in a wretched area, for wretched people. Flea pit would be a flattering description: not quite a dosshouse, but not far removed either. Smaller families lived in one room and the more affluent or bigger families enjoyed the luxury of two rooms. One cooking ring per habitation, one toilet facility down the hall for each floor. No complaints from us children: after all, it was impossible to wash with any regularity. That's where we were to live for several months, if you could call this living! Food was extremely scarce. Even so, heartbreaking pride compelled the mothers to go through the pretence of cooking, so that the neighbours could not measure the depths of one's degradation. They maintained this frequent charade by boiling pots of water and each one thought the rising steam would deceive the others into believing that they were actually cooking a meal.

At least, we always had company at night: when we returned to our rooms and switched on the lights, our visitors were waiting ... bugs! The beds were covered, totally covered, in bugs! No matter how many there were, they always disappeared instantly; but on waking up in the mornings, there was plentiful evidence of their presence, in the marks on our bodies and the blood-spots on the sheets. Yet even that we almost became used to, as well as the battalions of cockroaches for, despite it all, we children – there must have been hundreds of us, or surely it just felt like that to the grownups – we children managed to enjoy ourselves. The entire building, all six floors of it, was our hunting ground. Up and down the stairways, in and out of empty bedrooms, playing every kind of devilish game that young minds can devise. That included the discovery of the most popular game of all: "Doctors and Nurses". Most favoured by the boys, still it was well and generously supported by many of the girls, and proved to be my enthralling initiation into the mysteries of the female body. No shortage of rooms to use as "hospitals", and no shortage of volunteer patients. The slightly older boys and girls were the ringleaders, but we were all ready to pitch in! In matters of dare-devilry I was, like John, one of the leaders. My best stunt was a precarious balancing act on a concrete ledge jutting out from the sixth floor of the building overlooking the street. I was applauded by my peers but had I fallen off, my parents would have killed me ...

Despite, or perhaps because of, our grim circumstances, we kids were mollycoddled quite a lot. We might so easily have developed into little gangsters and some of us probably did.

School in Paris was a clear indication of Mother's softness towards us: for just as I had loved school in Lunéville, I hated it here. The building itself was grim and grimy and so was the teacher. I loathed and feared him with all my being and he didn't particularly cherish me either. It was a war of attrition; a stand-off. I had by then been re-elevated to my proper class level and found it tough going. The outcome was that on many mornings I cultivated an imaginative variety of ailments like toothaches, headaches, stomachaches and more. Had I known about leprosy then, I would have claimed that too. Whatever I pretended, Mother chose to believe me and always allowed me to take the day off. Her notes to the teacher were greeted with justified cynicism and my relationship with school and teacher naturally deteriorated by leaps and bounds, but my knowledge of Paris grew in inverse ratio. I had a best friend from Budapest called Ludi, short for Ludovic, and with or without him, I began to discover the city. Mostly alone of course, because he was quite properly at school.

Paris was the most exciting place in the world and it was all there just for me. Daily, I walked miles and miles. Clearly, I had no money. I rode public transport by telling outrageous lies about having lost my fare. There was always a sympathetic passenger or conductor who helped me on my way. For refreshment, I would stop at bars and beg a glass of water which was sometimes accompanied by the gift of something more solid. Thus, I bummed my way around the city and in the process, developed a genuine interest in historic buildings. I visited Notre Dame, the Pantheon, the Sacré Coeur, the Étoile, the

Eiffel Tower, and above all, the Dôme des Invalides. Napoleon's tomb and the battle flags clustered around it gave my imagination the most wonderful scope. I fought those battles, I really did! Many other buildings I visited, both inside and out, and finally I got to the Louvre. Was it unusual for a ten-year-old boy to stand there alone gazing awe-struck at the Mona Lisa? It was a magic time of adventure which helped to get me away from our flea pit. My French had improved considerably, and I encountered exciting people and had great escapades.

If memory serves, Celia was attending school more assiduously than I, but I have a sneaking feeling that John was beginning to be a bit of a handful, and not always easy to control. Still, he was my hero and protector. By then fifteen or sixteen years old, whatever he said was a mighty truth.

Chapter 8

Meantime our position had continued to deteriorate. The French police must have felt that we were not sufficiently persecuted, because about now they started to raid the hotel at frequent but irregular intervals. *Les flics* swaggered up in their swish uniforms and demanded to see everyone's documents. Absence or irregularity of identification led to the immediate arrest of the head of the family.

And irregularities, of course, there were in plenty. The men would be taken away and then returned a day or two later, diminished in stature and self-confidence and with even emptier pockets.

The nightmare conditions being experienced by Jewish refugees at the hands of the French authorities have been sympathetically and very accurately portrayed in a book by Erich Maria Remarque, entitled *Arch of Triumph*. If it were still available, it should be made prescribed reading.

At about this time of increased official pressure, my parents found an organisation that helped refugee children by placing them with concerned and generous families in Switzerland for a limited period. This gave the children much needed holidays and at the same time allowed a period of respite for the parents. And so, in no time at all, Celia and I found ourselves on a train to Switzerland, on our way to a village called Roggwil, near Langenthal, in the province of Berne. Celia was to spend her four weeks with a spinster school-mistress who owned a big house of her own on the edge of the village. She was very ancient: probably at least thirty-five years old, pretty of face and very kind. Meantime, I was sent to the house of the village treasurer (*Gemeindekassier*) Mr Hönger. He, his wife and

34

their two sons made me extremely welcome. I stood outside their immense, magnificent chalet and thought: "How can people get to live in palaces like these?" Of course, size is relative; I was small, so the house appeared huge. When I revisited as an adult, many years later, the chalet had shrunk! Frau Hönger and the family and the house immediately enfolded me in their warmth. I don't know what got hold of me then. Here I was in paradise, and I promptly turned into a whingeing monster. I decided that I was suffering from homesickness, and started to cry and scream and have tantrums. The kindness and patience shown by the Höngers did not get through to me. Admittedly, it was the first time away from our parents, but Celia also got infected by my malaise, and promptly developed the same tantrums there at the other end of the village. For my part, I wrote at least twice-daily letters to my parents in Paris, accusing the Höngers of every kind of brutality and wickedness that my febrile brain could invent. In all this, for five days and nights, I was fully supported by Celia.

Then suddenly, one fine day, the Hönger family took us both on a surprise trip to a village not far away. We arrived at a beautiful mansion surrounded by magnificent grounds. In the middle of the grounds there was a little lake. And there, sitting at the edge of the lake with his feet dangling in the water and a fishing rod clutched in both hands, sat my friend Ludi! The beneficiary of a scheme similar to ours, he had embraced the opportunity with both arms and was having, in modern parlance, a ball. He had found his bowl of cherries. This had an instant effect upon me. My screaming stopped at that very instant. So did Celia's. We had a lovely afternoon in Ludi's garden, and returned to Roggwil two much-changed children. Once we allowed ourselves to do so, we had a great time. The people, the village, the weather, the children we met, the food (above all, the food!) were all wonderful. We had great outings and became acquainted with lovely parts of Switzerland. I met the Höngers' friends and everyone was incredibly sympathetic and kind. Many of them had taken in children similarly placed. The chalet I lived in was comfortable and homely. The only drawback was that I had to share a bed with Hansi, the younger boy. A few years my junior, he was an enthusiastic bed-wetter. Thanks to him, we both woke up soaking wet in the mornings and he did his damnedest to blame me for his efforts at irrigating the mattress, bless his little heart. I should be grateful that I did not develop chronic rheumatism in my left leg! Despite his protestations of innocence, I don't think his parents were fooled for a minute.

Somewhere about the middle of my stay they told me they had suspected that I had been writing a pack of lies to Paris during those first few days. Mr H had steamed open my letters and inserted notes of his own to reassure my mother. I must admit, it had surprised me at the time that her replies to me were not more solicitous. No fools they, the Höngers!

All good things must come to an end. The holiday that gave everybody nightmares to begin with had turned from frog to prince. The time had come to go home to Paris and we viewed our return with mixed emotions. But back to Paris it was. We were taken to the railway station at Berne and for the second time in a few weeks made our journey, this time in reverse, across the Franco-Swiss border and home to the family. Quite the seasoned travellers!

Chapter 9

OUR RECEPTION in Paris was naturally very warm, but it was cooled a bit by the return to the same old misery. As was no doubt intended by the French authorities, conditions had become abysmal. Unknown to us children, plans were afoot for us to migrate further, and my parents soon began a new correspondence with the Höngers in Switzerland who offered to take us in again in the event of my parents' imminent removal. In the meantime, we were back at school in Paris. In my case, the relationship with the teachers remained as before, horrific, as did my attendances. I continued my love affair with Paris, and at least strove to improve my knowledge of French. The only thing that relieved the drabness of the XIII Arrondissement was a park near us called Monsouris and I played there quite a lot with the other savages from the hotel. We also pursued the indoor sports I mentioned earlier, with unflagging enthusiasm.

There was another pastime on my peregrinations about Paris. In those days, the gutters were constantly being washed by generous flows of water and I would throw painted corks into those exciting streams and follow them wherever their rushing course took them. This was often for great distances. If a cork occasionally got snagged, I would free it and continue to follow its bobbing journey. Thus I was led to quite a few unknown segments of the city and among them the Quartier Juif (the Jewish Quarter). I remember it well. On the rare occasions we could afford to shop in the grocery stores there, I would stand behind Mother, my mouth watering, inhaling the scents of the *schmaltz* herrings and *haimishe* cucumbers in their barrels of brine. I can still smell them now. The shops were invariably on the ground floor of tenement buildings and I recall with pure joy the best example of fractured French that I have ever heard: a *Mammeh* shouting from a top floor as her son came hurtling down the stairs four at a time: *"Oy Gevalt! Fall mir nisht die escalliers herub!"* This suffers in the translation. Basically, the meaning was "Don't fall down the stairs", but the sentence was made up of a wonderful mixture of Yiddish and French. This is just one example of how Yiddish becomes merged with the language of the countries in which it is being spoken. Oh Paris!

Back to my corks: I even gave them names, like "Prince" and "Student" and "Hero" and they were great companions on my lonely but exciting outings. Fantastic adventures, and what mystery and fun!

This was still the year 1934, and back in Nazi Germany the terror was mounting. As I mentioned before, it was the year of the "Night of the Long Knives", the year when Hitler had his showdown with Roehm and his Brownshirts. Further excuses for bloodshed and horror! And the Jews' sufferings continued to grow. They were to blame for everything. At the time, there was a common saying in Germany: *"Die Juden und die Radfahrer"*. "For everything, blame the Jews and the cyclists."

Chapter 10

IN THE LATE SUMMER of 1934, my Uncle Victor decided to follow in my father's footsteps and leave Germany. Not before time! He hoped to establish a foothold in England and chose a town called Nottingham, where he had relatives and friends. He too had left his family behind to give him a chance to get settled. They would be following in 1935. On the way to England, he stopped off to see us in Paris. I remember his visit vividly, and my excitement at seeing him. I was climbing all over him, and drove him slightly crazy. In the end, he had to tell me to pipe down. *"Hack mir nisht in tchainick!"* ("Don't hit me in the tea kettle" or "Don't drive me up the wall".) I enjoyed hearing about my cousins Joe and Manfred. Joachim was to become "Joe" when he arrived in England later, whereas Manfred loyally stuck to his given name when all about him were changing theirs after the fashion of the time. Although most refugees spoke atrocious English, they thought they would not be recognised as refugees if their names sounded English.

Victor's sojourn in Paris was very short but he, my Aunt Gina and the boys were to become an important part of my life some years on and to this very day.

Earlier I made reference to renewed contacts with the Höngers in Switzerland. They, as well as Celia's lady teacher, were happy to extend to us more of their kind hospitality and this time for a longer period, while my parents moved to Italy. My memories of the Jack Kutners at this period are a bit vague and I do not remember them being in Paris with us, but my guess is that they had gone from Lunéville to Italy direct and it may well be for this reason that my father chose Italy as our next destination. Or maybe because Italy was still generous in accepting refugees from Germany. Whatever our parents' motivations, Celia and I soon found ourselves reunited with our Swiss friends. It was winter and the village looked wonderful in its covering of snow. The Höngers were kinder than ever. At weekends, they taught me the rudiments of skiing on the big slope at the back of their house.

But it was not to be all play. We had to resume our schooling and thus I started my fifth school in under two years and in my third country. Here the language was German. Of course, that presented no problems for me or Celia. Just the same, back I had to go to primary one, to enable me to catch up with the other more parochial subjects: Swiss customs, History, Geography, and the awful Switzerdütsch. This time, school was nearly all bliss. The teachers were kind and understanding and I got on well with my schoolmates. We sat in a bright airy building and I responded well to these pleasant conditions, but not before Herr H. had put me through the traumatic experience of giving me a horrendous pudding-basin haircut. Was I mortified! Fortunately, I wore one of those knitted caps with pom-pons which are fashionable again now and this helped conceal the disaster. Now eleven years old, I was beginning to be sensitive about my appearance and becoming aware of friendly glances from some of the girls at school. I felt totally ridiculous and indeed, I looked it. Consequently, I was reluctant to take off my cap even in the classroom. It took a full lifetime for my hair to grow back!

Our stay continued into the early summer of 1935. We again went on trips to different friends and places. Once, we were invited to lunch at a friend's house in the Bernese Oberland and I was urged to partake heartily of a meal which included swedes, smothered in a rich creamy sauce. The minute the first mouthful crossed my lips, I knew that swedes and I were destined to be mortal enemies. Out of innate politeness, I tried to force down as much of the awful goo as I could, but suddenly had to leave the table, race out of the house, and there, leaning against the wall, puke up a white, undigested mess onto the beautifully manicured garden. My contribution to Swiss horticulture! Palefaced, I went back into the house. The hosts took one look at me and, convinced that I had been upset by the journey, insisted that I take more food to rebuild my strength. Promptly they served up more of the same. Disaster! This time, I puked it all over the table! I have never eaten the foul stuff since. However, swedes and pudding-basin haircuts and occasional bedwettings (courtesy of Hansi) apart, this stay in Switzerland was marvellous. It did not seem that six months had passed when the call came to rejoin our parents, this time in Milano, Italy.

Book 3
Italy

Chapter II

MY PARENTS had made their move from France while we were farmed out in Switzerland and they had temporarily rented a very pleasant furnished apartment in Milano. Goodness knows where the money came from. Once again, a joyful reunion! There is one thing about painful separations: you can mostly look forward to joyful reunions. Perhaps I should qualify that: it was only my mother who came to meet us at Milano's Central Station. My father could not be there as he was already up to his neck in developing his new factory. John was absent because he was still at some kind of technical high school in the Massif Central in France. He had been sent there even before Celia and I left for Switzerland and would be joining us in Italy some months later. I wonder how my parents afforded his stay there but it certainly gave him a good technical grounding, which would stand him in good stead years later.

To return to our arrival in Milan. After our living accommodation in Paris, anything would have seemed good and this sunny, furnished place certainly did. The landlady greeted us warmly and Mother acknowledged it by saying, "*Grazie tante.*" I could not understand why Mother called her "Aunt"!

Once again, I was sent back to school. The Ginnasio Giosué Carducci was a fine old High School about fifteen minutes walk from where we lived. Yes, you are right! I had to start again in a very much lower class, because, yes, I had to adapt to the Italian educational environment. That is to say, I now had to learn additional subjects such as Italian History and Culture, Geography, and of course, the Italian language. By now I was getting quite inured to having to work my way up the ladder, and I had no trouble at all in assimilating Italian. Having arrived in the spring, I spent the remaining few weeks of the school year in the bottom class. By the following year, I was promoted back to my proper level and came out top in Italian! What the Hell – if I don't blow my own trumpet, nobody will!

In that first full year I began to make quite a few friends and as I write this, Leopoldo Pirelli, classmate, is one of the great names in Italian industry. Because he was a rich man's son, we scrounged from him shamelessly. Footballs and all kinds of sports equipment were an expected tribute. Looking at a class photograph of the middle thirties, I identify other friends: Guido Marchetti; Lincoln Massone; Enrico Loiacono, son of a Secretary of State in Mussolini's Fascist government, the ugliest and most unfortunate looking little boy I have ever seen (his ears were the prototypes on which Walt Disney's Dumbo was modelled); and Sergio Diena, scion of a distinguished Jewish Italian family. I must not forget Bruno Minuto, small and very good looking. He attracted the perverts in great numbers and once was attacked by a man near Milan's Central Station, which created a great outcry. Near the Carducci there was a school stationer's shop, owned by an "unfrocked" school teacher. They eventually got him closed down, as he tried to have a go at most of us boys from time to time. I remember him well; he was always giving us little gifts. I might well have been offended if he hadn't had a go at me too.

In my form we also had some very nice girls, in particular Elena Aresi and Maddalena Bilesio. They were an important part of my Italian school years and they were to remain good companions during my formative period in Italy.

A brief mention is necessary of the teachers who were in charge of my education in the Ginnasio: Mlle. Bassi, who kept my French alive and interesting; Signa. Rabitti-Ferraris, a fat cow with a pretentious name who succeeded in making me hate maths from the instant that she set foot in our classroom: I did not even slice open the pages of my textbook for the whole of that year! In those days textbook pages were not always cut. I suppose it was for economy reasons. And then there was the one and only Prof. Rossi, my principal teacher. He was a giant of a man among the toadying, sycophantic, servile, Fascist pygmies who called themselves teachers at that time. It was a kind of repetition of Nazi Germany: the teachers held on to their jobs by their subservience to the System. All blessings flowed from Mussolini and we were the willing, malleable targets of this method of education. Apart from this political aberration, however, I do think the standards were quite high and at that time we Jewish immigrants were still treated as equals and given an even chance to shine,

Italy in 1934 and 1935 was very much dominated by the dictator Mussolini. Since his March on Rome, Il Duce had established himself Master of Italy's destiny. He had even created a Fascist calendar, dating from his accession to power in 1922. He aped the ancient Romans in many things, including the progressive numbering of each year since his accession to power as Year of the Fascist Era I, II, III and so on, much as the Romans had done. Thus 1934, the year of our arrival, was Anno XII. His identification with the "Glories of Rome" was pretty evident in everything he did. He renamed the Mediterranean *"Il Mare Nostro"* and the French town of Nice was only allowed to be referred to as Nizza, because of the man 's immense territorial ambitions which linked Nice with Corsica and Tunis, as well as Abyssinia, as the first steps in his plans for rebuilding the *Impero Romano*. The adoration he received from the people had to be fed by proclamations such as this and promises, promises, promises. I thought it necessary to give some of this background because it was to affect our lives considerably and indeed those of many other Jews who had settled in Italy, in particular from Germany.

Following Mussolini's senseless decision to invade Abyssinia in 1935, to atone for an Italian failure there around the turn of the century, the lifestyles of all Italians suffered from his imperialist dreams. There was certainly little chance of deriving any great gain from this brutal aggression. But it gave Mussolini's controlled newspapers many opportunities of mouthing loudly about "The reborn glories of Rome" (*Roma rivendica l'Impero*), "The Empire resurrected", and of course, "*Il Duce*". What this surge of national fervour did to the poor, primitive Abyssinians has been very well documented elsewhere. Primitive though they were, they almost fought the Italian juggernaut to a standstill with their lances. They were bombed to hell, they were crushed by tanks, yet it took Mussolini one year to reach the capital Addis Abeba. What this demonstrated unequivocally was that the Italians were and are lousy soldiers.

On the home front, the Italian people had to undergo many discomforts and privations. We suffered many shortages. All were expected to have their iron railings demolished to help build tanks, and to hand over all personal jewellery (not that we, the Kutners, had any) to support the war effort. You arrived at school clutching your meagre contribution and there in the courtyard stood four Fascists in their gaudy uniforms, each holding one of the corners of a large sheet into which you placed your goodies. In general, an austerity life-style was introduced. However, despite all I have said until now, no one should be fooled into thinking that I and John, who had not so long since returned from France, were not caught up in the youthful euphoria engineered by the massed publicity of the Fascist Regime.

Through school, I was obliged to join the Balilla which was the boy's branch of the Fascist Movement: a mixture between Boy Scouts and (heaven forgive me) Hitler Youth. But really there no comparison with Hitler's louts. The organisation was quite benevolent. The uniforms were gorgeous. I cannot pretend that I didn't enjoy it. There I was in my pretty fez, marching with my peers, singing outrageously patriotic songs, again dedicated to the greater

Balilla Uniform

glory of Rome, and Italy, and Il Duce. My brother found it convenient to join a slightly senior arm of this Heldenspiel. And boy, did he look superb! Forage cap, rakishly poised on brilliantined hair, a Clark Gablish moustache, epauletted black jacket, cinched in at the waist, riding-breeches and black boots. Later, for the hell of it, he became a glider pilot and was able to add wings to this dashing outfit. My uniform consisted of black fez, black shirt, blue kerchief held together by a Mussolini badge, short pants, and the whole thing completed by a broad, black cummerbund. I was twelve years old, and for a little while it was great fun. There was absolutely no hoodlumism; it would simply not have been countenanced.

Nevertheless, with the outbreak of the Spanish Civil War in 1936, to which Italian troops (and in particular the Airforce) contributed so "heroically", I found myself very quickly seeing the light. So did my brother. The Italians and the Germans on the one side, supporting "El Caudillo", Franco, and the Russians on the opposite side, were using the Spanish war as a rehearsal for bigger and better things to come. The people at home were again being fed the usual claptrap. In a small, careful way, John and I began to express critical views of the situation, and I was quite frequently reprimanded at school. Never by Prof. Rossi, but the headmaster threatened me with expulsion. It turned out he was only a little ahead of events.

Chapter 12

A S I HAVE SAID, this was about 1936, and it was the time when I began to understand that my father, who was slaving his heart out for us, was a very sick man. By now he had established his factory "Unitas" and he was permitting himself to work no more than fourteen hours a day. My mother, or we children, protesting loudly, carried his hot lunch to him daily in a shopping bag; a long walk from our fairly recently rented flat in Via Plinio. Way back in Paris, or was it even in Germany? he had discovered a small lump on a testicle. But of course, there was no time to pursue the matter. Making a *parnusse*, a living, for the family, was the Number One Priority. No time for fripperies and frivolities such as ill health. By now, however, the lump was getting bigger and painful and eventually it was diagnosed as cancer. Still he had found no time for an operation, but by 1936 it was clear that without surgery he would not survive. Yet he kept on working. At Unitas he had a partner, one Mr Brenner, who certainly did not put in the hours my father did. I imagine he had supplied the capital for this struggling enterprise. In any event, one day the Fascist Secret Political Police came to the factory, searched my father's desk, and removed some "seditious propaganda". With it, they also removed my father. Strangely, Herr Brenner was nowhere to be seen. They kept my father, my poor completely apolitical father, in jail for almost two weeks on totally trumped-up charges. All he ever knew was trying to keep his business going and feeding the family. Politics? What on earth was politics? Mr Brenner, however, if not political, must certainly have been an opportunist, for we were sure he had arranged the whole thing. So, instead of walking my father's lunch to the factory, we now walked it daily to the prison.

The prison, with its horrendous dictatorship-style conditions, was no spa. My father's health deteriorated even more rapidly, but at least Mr Brenner's ploy did not work and he did not get rid of him. After Dad's release Brenner quickly disappeared from the scene. John then joined the firm as an outside rep. As in Lunéville, the customers were mainly market traders. To get paid by them, you first had to catch them. It was apropos a particularly slow payer that I first heard my father's immortal expression: *"A lange Krenk is a gewisser Toit."* (A long illness is a sure death.) How prophetically appropriate! Anyway, I recall that after a long time, that customer did a runner and we never did get paid. My poor brother was often subjected to a lot of abuse for his alleged incompetence as a salesman but then, where could he find time to gain experience? He was much too busy taking care of his large group of adoring girlfriends.

By late 1936 Dad was noticeably worse. An operation was arranged. The date was fixed. Thanks to my mother's unbelievable ability to con people into anything, the great Professor Donati had agreed to perform the operation for nothing, of course. My father reluctantly went into hospital, but how could the business survive without him? On the eve of the operation, he discharged himself. No amount of hand-wringing on my mother's part could change his mind. Priorities just were different then. So he kept getting worse.

Strange though that may seem, family life had continued fairly normally in that year. My parents kept worrying and providing, my brother kept chasing the girls and selling a few Unitas shirts, and I continued at school. My biggest worry was that my parents could not afford to buy me a bicycle. I was clearly being made to suffer from an unjust deprivation. I did continue to spend time with my friends, and we developed a game in which we played proper eleven-a-side football with inverted metal bottle caps, into which we inserted little round discs of paper painted with the colours of the various football teams. These bottle caps were flicked with the finger tips in pursuit of an improvised ball. We played this game interminably on carpets and floors and were forever being chased by our mothers. I recall that we even had complete league tables for home and away matches. Was this the fore-runner of Subbuteo? The funny thing is, I cannot remember what we used for a ball.

We played real football, of course, in public parks or wherever. Despite being the worst player in the team (it was called M.A.S. – *Memento Audere Semper*), I managed to get myself elected captain. I must have bullied myself there. Seldom the best at anything, but always in charge! One exception: I was a fairly good middle distance runner and managed to achieve some mild distinction in youth championships. But I never learned to swim! We had a "Street Gang" and there too I was head honcho, followed by my deputy honcho, Sergio Diena. He was fat, so for him it was a hard but rewarding life. Other pastimes: sneaking into the local cinema without ever paying (there was usually cabaret too and we really ogled those showgirls). And of course, we stunt-rode bicycles (other people's) at dangerous speeds wherever we were not supposed to be. But then we were not too welcome anywhere. We used to have competitions at balancing on railings to see who could stay up the longest, but one day while showing off I forgot to stay up and fell with my legs on either side of the railing. I was in excruciating agony and for weeks later very heavily bruised. I did not dare tell my parents and so I never saw a doctor and it took me years to convince myself that I had done no permanent damage. Ouch! How that memory hurts.

We were also becoming very much aware of the opposite sex. As part of our mutual instruction, my cousin Margot and I had some astonishing wrestling matches.

I have mentioned that the Jack Kutners had also moved to Milan and we saw each other a lot. Amongst a variety of jobs he held, Uncle Jack had become a wholesale rep for electric light bulbs. With his inimitable *chutzpa* (quite unlike my father) he would *schmoose* his way into the offices of the managing directors of the largest firms to sell his product. On occasion, he would take my brother along with him as "assistant". John said he had never seen anything like it! In a trice, Jack would have his shoes off and be standing on the director's desk in stockinged feet, inserting a bulb in the overhead socket to demonstrate the efficacy of his particular brand. Despite Jack's very broken Italian, he seldom failed to make a sale. What a guy! Alas, John never made it as an electric light salesman ...

In 1936 the family, minus Dad who was working, spent an idyllic holiday in the hills above Lake Como. We had rented rooms in a rambling nineteenth century farmhouse with massive beams and enormous stone walls. It was surrounded by fields as far as the eye could see and the sun quite definitely shone all the time. For a city boy like me it was paradise. Paradise or no, I did become indisposed for a couple of days and the doctor was called. He examined me and announced with an absolutely straight face: "Young man, of course you're not well! Your heart is on the wrong side!" And I really believed that for a long time afterwards. But anyway, he had me back on my feet the very day of his visit.

In this wonderful sleepy village which still induces a great nostalgic feeling, I met my first real girlfriend, fourteen-year-old Andreina, by my standards a mature older woman! The vast meadows in which we walked, discussing lofty subjects, helped to further the romance. In the evenings she would join us in organised hunts for the bats that lived in the tall old sheds. We did this by knocking them out of their low flight with long poles. I kept missing, but we had great fun. Romantic it wasn't, but every little bit helps. At least we were together a lot.

Chapter 13

So 1936 MOVED INTO 1937. The Abyssinian War was still being fought fiercely, Italy was going broke and we didn't have to try very hard to do the same. Naturally, Celia and I were still at school and I suppose I was a slightly above average student. By now I was of course fluent in three languages and had begun to study and enjoy Latin. What I still hated was maths and I was a disaster at science, art and music. With all my heart, I also detested the prospect of having to learn Hebrew in preparation for my Barmitzvah. But my father was adamant. Only about two months before the Barmitzvah was due to take place, I had to start a crash course of lessons. If I had known about Fagin then, I would probably have compared my Hebrew teacher with him. He may not have picked pockets, but he certainly picked his nose ... with dedicated concentration. He also looked the part: small eyes, long bony proboscis, straggly pointed beard, and talons for fingers. He had an inbuilt lack of charm. How I hated it when he touched me. But I hated and feared it even more when he reported my lack of application to my parents. Apart from any personal fear of punishment, I was also most reluctant to upset my father whose health was now galloping downhill. But he could still be firm and somehow he and my Hebrew teacher got me there.

My Barmitzvah took place in January of 1937. It was a small family party and I was allowed to ask a couple of friends. Apart from some moderate presents, the best thing to come out of that day was the fact that I never had to see my Hebrew teacher again.

I have made only passing reference so far to our flat in Via Plinio. It was two floors up in an oldish block, with one of those tiny, useless, railed balconies, but the flat was really quite spacious. My parents naturally shared a bedroom and so did my brother and I, whilst Celia had a room of her own. There were at least two public rooms and a fair-sized entrance hall. Plenty of room for my friends and me to play our games of football and get under everybody's feet.

It must have been around this time that I had to sit a series of important exams. I thought I was sailing through them, until the maths exam came up. There I froze. But totally! So I decided to pretend to faint. I just put my head down on my desk, let my arms dangle, and prayed someone would notice. Prof. Rossi was the invigilator. When he spotted my predicament, he got me water, tested my pulse and declared there might be a problem with my heart. I was sent home and later was allowed to take just my oral test, which I passed with flying colours. Virtue is its own reward?

As the year progressed, it became clear that my father simply must undergo surgery at once and so he went to hospital for a second time, to be operated upon by the very forgiving Professor Donati. We hated being made to visit the hospital. The ward was one of those real charity wards of old: narrow, very long, shabby and depressing, with cracked, discoloured white tiles. A urinal with beds! The smell of death clung to the room and most of the patients in it and the aroma of incontinence permeated the ward. Run by nuns in their ancient habits, it was a Last Stop nightmare. I have to report that the operation was a success, but the patient never recovered. Forgive my cynicism, but it had been a lost cause to begin with. The cancer had spread all over his body; looking at what remained of my father in that hospital bed was profoundly frightening.

Mother brought him back home. It would be nice if I could say that she had brought him home to end his days peacefully. In fact, he was in constant agony and his nightly screams became part of our lives. Day and night mother gave him painkilling injections (where did she get the stamina from?) but they helped little. Before our eyes, he faded away. One day in December 1937, I was visiting a friend's flat just

My parents with my sister, myself and a friend, 1937

around the corner. I had been told not to go far, because Dad was by now in a near-coma. In mid-afternoon, my brother called for me. I went alone into my parents' bedroom and held my father's hand. After some time, he opened his eyes. Still with his hand in mine, he smiled faintly and said, "Norbert." That was his last word ever. He died a few hours later. I still see him very clearly in that bed but find it too painful to describe how he looked. He was forty-seven.

And so we buried my father in the Jewish section of Musocco Cemetery in Milan. Those awful last years of his life had been dedicated to bringing up his family against all odds. Despite the losing uphill battle, he tried to provide for us and brought us up with justice and kindness. Would he have lived longer if circumstances had permitted him to take care of his health a little sooner? What I do know for certain is that I missed him dreadfully and it was many years before I stopped seeing him in the street.

My father's death had left us completely unprovided for. My brother struggled half-heartedly to continue selling some Unitas products, but his thoughts were elsewhere and his role of provider was irksome. He had other ambitions and desires and did not take easily to his new responsibilities. Mother found it necessary to sub-let the master bedroom and a sitting room to a refugee couple from Germany and their teenage daughter, Eva. I resented that they lived in my parents' bedroom and that Mother had to fetch and carry for them. On the other hand, our lodgers were wealthy in my eyes and quite generous. He was an alcoholic, but since he always asked me to take his refundable bottles back to the shop and didn't expect the return of the deposit money, I didn't care if he drank himself to death. Eva was the other compensation. She was pretty, sexy and friendly; probably one or two years older than myself. At the request of her parents, I gave her lessons in Italian, and was always well paid. But I would have taught her for nothing. She was a ray of sunshine and she had quite an exclusive place in my fantasies. Her parents were waiting for a "capitalist" visa to Palestine: suddenly they had it, and suddenly they were gone. No more lessons, no more income, and goodbye Eva.

Chapter 14

THE YEAR IS 1938: time to do a little stocktaking, to cast a look over my shoulder and review the political situation as it affected Jewish life in Italy and Germany and our own in particular.

My father's recent death had dealt a shattering blow to our family unit. He had always kept us together and in practical terms we were now rudderless, despite Mother's efforts. As an entity we started breaking up. My sister Celia left us during this year to go to England on a sponsored domestic scheme, which at least meant freedom for her. This scheme was salvation for many young people but in practical terms was not always adequately rewarded. So now we were three, and for us the year was turning into a catastrophe. Lest I give the wrong impression, previously there had also been some very happy times in Italy. That holiday in Como shaped my taste for future holidays: the long leisurely days, sun-baked fields, the lazy drone of insects, milk straight from cow or goat, long walks over gentle hills holding hands with a pretty girl.

The schooldays in Italy had also been good, as well as many of my friendships and the earlier good times with my father and mother when the family was still intact. In those years there had been enough to eat and we children were not too aware of the problems. The Italian people had been warm and friendly and did not really change all that much under the racist laws that were to come. And I thought Milano was great to grow up in.

Back to my Report: in 1936 Streicher had promulgated his ignominious Nuremberg race laws which had set the final seal of doom on the surviving Jews in Germany. If you had just a Jewish grandparent, you were classified as Jewish and legally open to all the persecution, hatred and excesses. These exploded into the ultimate horror of the cynically named *Kristallnacht.*

In Paris in 1938, a young Polish Jewish student by the name of Herschel Grynszpan assassinated a minor German diplomat, Von Rath. The shock waves instantly spread throughout Germany and a "spontaneous expression of the will of the German people" followed. In real terms, what took place was a highly efficient orchestrated night of savagery and violence, aimed at what remained of Jewish families, their possessions, their homes and their places of worship. From this appalling nightmare scenario the *Kristallnacht* received its name, the connotation being the smashed windows of all Jewish private property, businesses and synagogues. This night of unspeakable inhumanity and savagery was perpetrated by an allegedly civilised people; but again the world tut-tutted and sat back and watched. There were perhaps a handful in Germany who disapproved, but even they did not dare give conspicuous expression to their disapproval.

It was also in this year of 1938 that Hitler began to press strongly for the annexation of Austria to the Fatherland. As a result of a very popular plebiscite, the Austrians overwhelmingly voted to become German and Nazi. And so, at the head of his troops, Hitler drove into Vienna in his Mercedes, through streets lined by the cheering masses and the deed was done. One consequence was that Mussolini had Herr Hitler directly on his Alpine borders. He viewed this with mixed feelings, but made discretion the better part of his valour by strengthening his commitments and ties with Germany. Hitler immediately demanded the introduction of anti-Jewish laws in Italy. These were happily put in place by Count Ciano, foreign minister and son-in-law of Mussolini. Suddenly, a hitherto non-racist Italy was made aware of the Jewish "peril" in its midst.

It should be noted that the Italian people as a whole did not even know what antisemitism was. Their subsequent discrimination against Jews was thrust upon the majority of them. The most damaging laws to be introduced were against Jews who had immigrated into Italy since 1922. They had to quit the country within six months, leaving everything behind. Children of such families were instantly expelled from school. I was one of the victims. Aged fourteen and a half, I was instructed never to darken my school doorstep again. I took it very badly, but my little setback was hardly a major factor in the order of world affairs, for at this very time Hitler was browbeating Neville Chamberlain into surrendering Czechoslovakia to the Nazis. Mussolini was either present or behind the scenes at all three meetings that took place between Hitler and Chamberlain. He had in effect become Hitler's jackal. Much as he may have disliked it, he was to play that role for the rest of his time. As Hitler had demanded and obtained the Rhineland, the Sudetenland, Austria and latterly Czechoslovakia, so Mussolini continued to clamour for Corsica, Nice and Tunis. This was purely a sop to any further imperialist aspirations the Italian people might have entertained. It is scarcely to be wondered at that all these massive political and military manoeuverings made the Jewish problem in Italy shrink into the background. But it was no minor matter for us.

The enjoyment of my earlier membership of the Balilla Organisation had naturally faded totally and I was mature enough to have come to detest the Fascist posturing. All this despite the "glorious" experience of being patted on my fez-adorned head by Il Duce himself during a spectacular parade. "*Bravo,*" he had said, "*bravo ragazzo,*" and passed by. And the crowd chanted, "*Duce, Duce, Duce!*" This episode, ironically, was swiftly followed by my aforementioned dismissal from school. I was by then in my fourth year of senior studies, continuing at the Giosué Carducci and making a reasonable name for myself in my studies. Prof. Rossi was still my principal teacher. I have mentioned him before, but it was at this time of incipient persecution that he showed his character and courage. He wrote a letter to my home, a very dangerous thing to do at that time, in which he tried to comfort me on my dismissal from school. In it he also wrote a blistering attack upon the régime. In the wrong hands, that letter would have landed him in prison. I still have that letter! Alas, no one else raised a cry and most of my best school friends became much less assiduous in their friendship. Under the circumstances, it was really hard to blame them.

It had become urgently necessary that I find a job and Mother secured for me a position as errand boy/filing clerk in an old established Italian/Jewish house of commerce. The managing director, Signor Ugo Colonna, was a lovely man, the only person I can actually remember who always wore real pince-nez. The job itself has faded into oblivion, except for two members of the staff: Signora Mombelli (it ought to have been Montibelli because of the magnificence of her breasts!) had a powerful effect upon my febrile adolescent imagination, thanks to the lavishly pointed display of those assets. Her kindness to me contrasted vividly with the attitude of the chief clerk who hated me with a passion. Interesting point: I remember the name of the lady with the breasts, but not the name of the chief clerk. When national edict decreed that all immigrant Jews be dismissed from their jobs, it was this very chief clerk who gloated on giving me the glad tidings. He wore the same look of relish as that displayed by the Nazi teachers in Germany and some of the Fascist teachers in Italy.

So there I was, out of work again. Of course it is not totally unthinkable that I was actually useless in my job. It's just easier to say that the chief clerk was a Fascist antisemite. What little income I earned was vitally necessary to us. Apart from Mother taking in lodgers, we had practically no money coming in. Celia had left, and my brother was mainly occupied elsewhere. At this time, I had to develop a very refined talent for shopping on credit. Actually, that had started during the latter stages of my father's illness. I would go to the grocer's next door, list in hand, and make my selections. When they were all carefully wrapped, and not before, I would trot out my excuses: "Forgotten my money", "Mother not home yet", "Father ill in bed" and so on. For some time my apparent wide-eyed innocence worked, but then I would find it expedient to move on to pastures new. Another street, another grocer, but the same tale. The sad part was that I could never again go back to the previous grocer who had befriended me. I am still a little ashamed, but ain't life like that ... a veritable minefield of shattered principles ... So we eked out our poor living, helped not a little by me and my selective shopping.

With her ingenuity and resourcefulness, my mother managed to pull more strings that led to another job for me: the same sort of work as the previous one, which anyway had only lasted a couple of months, but this time for the Milan Committee for Jewish Refugees. This would bring about a dramatic turning point in my life and I shall have more to say about that later but meanwhile, concurrently with my sacking from school and my first job, John had begun to take a greater and more brotherly interest in me. He started taking me to the open-air Opera, he queued with me for the Gods at La Scala to hear Gigli, he told me about some of his girl friends and even took me on (borrowed) bicycle rides. Just the way a big brother should. Then one day, not long after, he just disappeared! At that time, it was totally impossible for a Jew with a Polish passport, or indeed any passport, to escape from Italy and enter France legally. The French just did not want to know. And that is where my brother's paper trail of disasters began.

Many panic-stricken people who were afraid of being unable to meet the six month's emigration deadline that had been imposed on us all, had themselves smuggled illegally and at great cost and danger over the Alps and into France. For reasons of his own, John did just that. No mean feat and very dangerous! On arriving in Nice, he surrendered to the French Police and immediately volunteered to join the Foreign Legion. The French had no problem with that and he was duly sent to the Legion's recruiting depot where he was to sign up. Maybe at that point he had second thoughts, or maybe a French Intelligence Recruiting Officer approached him. In the event, he was enlisted as an undercover agent by the French and sent back to Italy to report secretly on Italian aircraft strength and other matters. End of Foreign Legion! Hail to the glamour of Espionage!

Having left illegally, he had no exit stamp from Italy in his passport, but did have a French entry stamp which he received on surrendering on the French side. Colossal error number one! In order to conceal his visit to France, the offending page with the stamp was torn out of his passport. Colossal error number two! Later, that missing page would prove hard to explain. However, back in Italy he started his earth-shattering activities, and for these he required my part-time help. So he enlisted me, a willing victim, as he no doubt also enlisted a squadron of girl-friends. Colossal error number three: hell hath no fury ...

For some time, John had become disillusioned with Fascist Italy and I feel sure that his new activity was inspired, at least in part, by anti-Fascist zeal. He had achieved some minor rank in his youth organisation and had already used his position there to disseminate anti-Fascist propaganda as best he could and there were quite a few who listened.

So John settled back home after France, if you could call it settling, and I became his trusted clerk. Picture the folly of all this: the two of us, Don Quixote and Sancho Panza, riding forth on our iron Rosinantes to unveil by ourselves the mysteries of the might of the Italian Airforce. John's preparation and briefing had been nothing short of ludicrous. He had been told to amass information and send it back to France by letter! We really did stupid things, like standing outside airports counting the number of military aircraft parked there. The letters in which he sent these stunning nuggets of useless information were in the shape of normal correspondence to a friend in France, leaving blank lines in between the written ones. These were to contain the secret information in invisible ink! Enid Blyton would have been ashamed of the maturity of this plot. However, the letters were duly sent, invisible ink and all; dictated by him and unfortunately written by me, complete with copies. These he "filed" in a box in his wardrobe containing business cards and envelopes! To this day I cannot fathom why he felt the need to store these documents. It was the beginning of the end. There was a genuine recipient in France who occasionally acknowledged or instructed by the same letter method. But when things went wrong, he simply ceased to exist. He had a very normal code name, which trembles on the tip of my tongue. The other thing I simply do not remember, or perhaps was never told, is how and where John received payment, if any. And so, he went on naively pedalling and peddling his scant, inaccurate, useless, childish information.

Naturally, Mother knew nothing of this so she was scared mindless when she received a phone call from one of my brother's superior officers in the Youth Organisation. The officer, probably one of those a little sympathetic to John's less than enthusiastic attitude to Fascism, asked if her son was at home and when she answered in the negative, he said, "Pack a case for him. At once! If and when he comes in, get him the hell out of the country! I have information that he is to be arrested on a very serious charge. And under no circumstances destroy any papers. If you do, you will be implicated. I won't be able to call you again." And with that he hung up. In the event, my brother John never did come home.

I came back very shortly after this highly dramatic call to find my mother absolutely paralysed by fear. First, you must picture the atmosphere of terror that permeated the whole of Mussolini's Police State: seditious talk and secret activities were punished by long prison terms or even death. So Mother's quaking fear could easily be understood. She had only just started trying to tell me what had happened when there was a very loud banging on our front door. I opened it to find three Secret Police standing there. They just brushed me aside and charged into the living room. My mother was told to remain seated and I was commanded to sit next to her. Two of the three agents stood over us. The third went straight to the wardrobe where my brother kept his papers. It was creepy! Without searching or hesitation, he took out the box of visiting cards and envelopes. This was the clearest possible indication that he was acting on information. Who supplied it still remains a mystery, although there was never any doubt in my mind that one of John's girlfriends was seeking revenge for some real or imaginary slight. Another case of hell hath no fury? I do know that at least one young woman was also arrested.

Thus, we came into the second phase of this bizarre, tragic episode. After quite some time, we had managed to discover where John was being held by the Authorities and were able to establish limited legitimate contact. The first thing my mother tried to do was to find a lawyer. This was certainly not made easier by the fact that lawyers did not wish to represent "Enemies of the State", nor did we have connections or funds to help us persuade them. In the meantime we kept receiving periodic visits from the Secret Police, mainly courteous, but always intimidating. They were looking for more information, but Mother knew nothing and in an awful fog of fear, I pretended total ignorance. I was not to get away with it!

There came the day when the police called for my mother and me and actually took us away for interrogation. It was the worst kind of hell. We were put into separate cars and taken to their headquarters where we were led to an intimidating interrogation room and made to sit at a table each. We both had a pad and pencil in front of us. An officer started dictating and we had to write, three times, every line he dictated. Of course, I instantly recognised extracts from the messages I had sent to France. Trying to disguise my hand-writing and even committing unusual spelling errors to lead their suspicions away from me proved to be a waste of time. There was no way, no hope of fooling them. At the end of a very long, gruelling session they told me with wide, happy grins, that they had recognised my handiwork from the beginning. Because of my age, they would not bring criminal charges against me but I would be required as a prosecution witness at my brother's trial! Mother was not implicated in any way, except that her passport as well as mine were sequestrated to prevent escape from Italy. All this because of what one might have thought to be a juvenile prank! But the horror was still unfolding ...

There followed a period of incredible strain for Mother. This was late 1938 and the trial was supposed to take place in the spring of 1939. The hunt for lawyers cost money we did not have, and it became necessary for us to give up our flat in Via Plinio, which in any case was only rented. As there were now only the two of us, we were able to move into lodgings consisting of just one room. No more floor-football games, no more childhood.

At the beginning of this narrative, I mentioned that after many years the truth might become slightly softened at the edges and the facts slightly blurred. I do wish I could invent some rear-sighted spectacles, so that I could look back over my shoulder and make such corrections as might prove necessary. But I can confirm that these would be few. Most of the facts are painfully engraved on my heart. There we were, the brilliant amateur spy master aged barely twenty, awaiting trial in a dank jail in Milan, and his little acolyte, not yet fifteen years old, in massive trouble with the Secret Police.

Chapter 15

ALL THIS TIME, I was trying to keep up my job at the Jewish Committee whilst Mother was moving heaven and earth to get me permission to emigrate to England. As the world knows, immigration permits were but a distant dream. That, in fact, was what the Milan Committee for Jewish Refugees was about. It existed to help people like us who were in desperate straits and also to create emigration possibilities. The chicken or the egg ... If you could get out of Italy leaving everything behind, you could not get in anywhere else. Or if by a miracle you received a permit to enter England, the French refused you a transit visa. Those lovely French!

So I did my filing and ran my errands, and met a lot of other people in distress, among them a family consisting of a lovely little girl of nine with her parents. They had established contact with an English couple called Reigate who were labouring from England to sponsor her. A visit from them was anxiously awaited in Milan, together with the British visa that would mean freedom, at least for the child. But the Reigates never arrived. In desperation, having quite given up hope, the family finally fled Milan with the intention of crossing the Alps illegally into France. Tragically, we never found out whether they made it. For all I know, in common with others, they may have perished in the attempt. And then, just a few days later, the Reigates did arrive, only to discover child and parents gone! Their precipitate departure was about to change my life; to give it a vital and desperately needed new direction. Someone at the committee had the brainwave of putting me forward to replace the little girl! My mother was of course consulted and of course she accepted enthusiastically, although it meant she would be left all alone in Italy.

The disappointed Reigates agreed to sponsor me in the girl's place and went back to the United Kingdom to start the necessary proceedings. The trouble was, I had no passport. So the amazing Mr Reigate came back to Milan and went with me to the British Consul who issued me with a British Government affidavit. A miraculous Open-Sesame! At one stroke, it opened up to me both the French and the British borders. We were all elated, but our celebrations, sadly, were premature.

Having said goodbye to my mother, Mr Reigate and I set out on our journey by train. We reached Bardonecchia on the Italo-French border, where there was the usual passport inspection. To our immense dismay I was hauled off the train, despite my precious documents. It appeared that my name was on the list of people not allowed to leave the country! I had not yet been cleared by the Italian authorities. Over Mr Reigate's fierce protestations, I was put in a cell, no joy at my age, whilst Mr Reigate regretfully had to travel on to the UK on his own, after waiting around for hours in vain.

That night in a cell was not to be recommended, but it certainly did help to round out my education. To coin a phrase, it was part of the rich tapestry of life and my life certainly contained a lot of rich tapestry. Mind you, that particular bit of tapestry I could have done without.

The following day I was freed and sent back to Milan, alone. Unexpected, I walked into our so-called apartment and gave my mother the second biggest shock of her life. She had, of course, thought me safely on the way to England. For my part, the disappointment and the ghastly sojourn in jail did nothing for my morale. We had been so confident that I had escaped the need to be a witness at John's trial.

When I went back to work at the Committee, I found that Mr Reigate had been in touch and it was agreed that his sponsorship would be kept in place once I obtained proper permission to leave Italy.

Selection of Passport pages showing Visa

John's trial was getting nearer and Mother was getting ever more frantic in her efforts to secure an effective defence for him. The other urgent need was the release of our previously much maligned Polish passports. So she used her good looks and cajoled and begged and bewitched, and lo and behold! two police officers called at our digs and gave us back those precious documents. This was in early 1939.

Now I had a passport and permission to enter England. What I did not have and could not get, was a transit visa through France, nor could I get another British affidavit. There was literally only one other way out to Britain: over the Brenner Pass, through Austria and Germany! Then Holland – a daunting prospect for a Jewish kid of fifteen. Sure of being turned down, I went to the German consulate full of trepidation, in search of a visa. Unlike the German passport, the Polish one carried no mention of religion, and to my relieved astonishment, I was granted permission to cross Germany. Indeed, with Teutonic charm, the consular official offered me a fortnight's holiday visa. Some chance! Hellfire would have held more appeal. Jews were being butchered in their thousands and he thought I should tour the country for pleasure! I just grabbed my transit visa and ran. And so, in April of the year 1939, at the age of fifteen and a quarter, having once again taken leave of my mother, I boarded the train and set forth alone, for England and a whole new chapter in my life.

Book 4
England

Chapter 16

ONE BOOK CLOSES, another opens. Before embarking on my journey to England, it is appropriate that I take stock once more. Now it is April 1939. Over the span of six years since January 1933, I have managed to escape Nazi Germany and its horrors. I have spent an unhappy year in France, followed by the good times in Switzerland. The Italian period which had started so well had descended to a fearful end via my father's wrongful imprisonment, which quite surely accelerated his agonising death. Of course, I shall never know whether his health was already impaired when we left Germany. Might he have been saved, had not all those migrations followed? The arrest and long-term incarceration of my dashing, handsome brother and the total dispersal of our family brought that period to its nadir. My father dead, my brother in prison, my sister in domestic service in England and my mother marooned in Italy, fighting a desperate rearguard action. Her only support was Uncle Jack, also trying to resist the terrible conditions. Your humble reporter, full of trepidation mingled with hope, was on his way to a new life in Britain.

So that was our situation. As for the global view, during this whole period, the Western World, and in particular Europe, had endured with admirable fortitude and equanimity the more or less contemporaneous emergence and rule of four of the most ferocious dictators in history. First, Mussolini in Italy, then Stalin in Russia, Hitler in Germany, and more recently, Franco in Spain. I have already alluded to the political changes taking place on the Continent, mainly brought about by Hitler, with the help of his jackal Mussolini. Now the stage was set for the confrontation that followed. Chamberlain, the British

Prime Minister, and his team of incompetents, having three times failed to satisfy Hitler at meetings in Germany in 1938, were still abasing themselves and humbling poor little Czechoslovakia, by running back and forth from London to Berchtesgaden and Berlin, mouthing "Peace in our time"! Well, "Peace in our time" was to be very shortlived. We were stung by the nettle from which we "plucked the flower, safety"! World War II began just weeks later. Meantime, the Jewish situation in Germany and Italy was largely and carefully ignored throughout the world.

Thus it happened that, having bidden my mother a tearful farewell and clutching passport and tickets in my sticky hand, I found myself on my way to the Brenner Pass and ultimate freedom. The word "Freedom" really did have a very tangible meaning for me. Thanks to the Police States I had lived in, I was in constant terror of all and every kind of officialdom, to the point of even being fearful of asking an ordinary policeman for directions. Add to this the persecution by the Italian State Police and my several arrests and interrogations and it can readily be understood how I felt about getting the hell out. There was also the little matter of being able at last to speak my thoughts without being punished or ostracised, But not quite yet! The Brenner Pass loomed! This border station between Italy and Germany was hopefully to be my last obstacle. I arrived there in the evening with the equivalent of a few shillings to my name and a sad little package of personal possessions. The border militia were making their way along the train towards me but I had no serious fears. Did I not have my beautiful legal papers? So when the officials reached me, it came as a staggering blow to be arrested once again and taken off the train, under guard. It appeared that my name had not yet been taken off the proscribed list. I tried to explain that the situation had been changed and that I was cleared to leave the country. Nothing helped. I was shoved into a room, carefully locked, while the border police sought enlightenment from Milan HQ. This was not quickly forthcoming and a cell was provided for me in which to spend the night. Prison cells were becoming a Kutner way of life: not one that I particularly appreciated. The border militia were mainly quite decent and were pleased to take most of my "capital" to buy me chocolate.

To the disappointment of the one thoroughly unpleasant officer who really gave me a hard time and peppered his conversation with the frequent use of the word "*Ebreo*" (Jew), I was cleared the next day and sent on my way, now twenty-four hours behind schedule.

Straight from the frying pan into the fire! For after this ordeal, here I was on a train in Nazi Germany, in my nice comfortable window seat, facing a bullet-headed gentleman sporting a swastika badge. The badge brought back many frightening memories of my earlier childhood years in Germany and I was inwardly quaking. Yet all he did was offer me sandwiches and interminable chat on the beauties of the Fatherland. I accepted the sandwiches with alacrity, all the time wondering what would happen to his pretty speeches if he knew I was a Jew. At least he could not take back the sandwiches, could he? Strange though it may seem, the trip was very pleasant and in time the train reached the Dutch border, The incubus was lifted! Finally, I was away from it all, into Holland. Some Dutchman approached me and said that since my last few pennies would be useless in Holland, I should give them to him and he would run and buy some chocolate for me. Run he did, come back he did not. Now I was truly penniless. And the train moved on. Some final memory!

At last, The Hook of Holland, the Channel Crossing and Harwich, England! Mighty, remote, unattainable England! Freedom!

Chapter 17

THE TRAIN FROM HARWICH was speeding towards Liverpool Street Station in London. The mighty adventure had begun! I can only conjecture as to the thoughts that must have tumbled around in my brain during that brief journey. Of course, I had some in-built, preconceived notions of what to expect from England and its people. I did not speak one single solitary word of English, but knew with absolute certainty that the principle that guided the British people's every waking moment was: "Ze time is ze money." With equal certainty, I knew that Englishmen were all "chentlemen", invariably wore tweed suits and brogues, had thick moustaches, and smoked pipes. They were cool and remote. In fact, they all looked and sounded like Anthony Eden, The women were distant, unapproachable and virginal. They wore cardigans, pearl necklaces, tweed skirts and thick stockings. The country was incredibly wealthy and so were most people in it. I suppose my whole juvenile thinking was a kind of M'lord and M'lady syndrome: an unshakable belief in the superiority of the English people.

Be that as it may, twenty-four hours late I arrived at Liverpool Street Station, tired, famished and penniless. It should have been no surprise that there was no one at the station to meet me, yet against reason, I was desperately disappointed. I had had no means of advising the Reigates of my late arrival and so, kindly picture the situation: not a word of English, literally not a penny in my pocket, no one to greet me, and thousands of strangers rushing about their business and ignoring this newly arrived fifteen-year-old foreign boy in his cheap knickerbocker suit and ankle socks, looking forlorn and bewildered. I did have Mr Reigate's telephone number, but no one to communicate it to. Wandering up and down the platform, I had spotted various people wearing Star of David armbands, which very reasonably led me to assume that they represented some kind of Jewish Aid Organisation. I approached them, but right away the language problem reared its head. Attempts to speak to these volunteer officials in German, French or Italian failed dismally. Then I had a brainwave: Why not try Yiddish?! My Yiddish wasn't all that good and still isn't, but I had learned some at my parents' knees and it certainly did open the conversational floodgates. I explained my situation which I am sure was a daily occurrence for them. They took me to a room and fed me sandwiches whilst someone contacted Mr Reigate's office.

When he was eventually reached, my arrival came as quite a surprise to him. He had just about given me up. I was taken to a Shelter for Refugees in the East End of London where I was to spend the night, sharing one large room with several other down-and-outs. One sharp memory: the sheets were so old and brittle that my feet went right through them and I slept in a nightmarish tangle, afraid that the Authorities at the shelter would discover the damage I had done and I would be suitably punished. However, no-one said an unkind word and about ten a.m. Mr Reigate's chauffeur-driven limousine arrived. Miracle of miracles! Such opulence I had never even visualised! Then, on the way to his office, I was able to admire in speechless astonishment the wonders that this part of London presented. I was overwhelmed by the red double-decker buses, the enormous hoardings which carried advertisements such as: "Guinness is good for you, just see what Toucan do," and "Stick no Bills, stick Watneys". Though I did not understand a word then, they evidently stuck in my memory for ever. A much-too-short journey in his sumptuous car saw me delivered to Mr Reigate's office, somewhere in East London where he was head of a large textile export/import agency.

I had to wait in an anteroom for quite some time, but eventually, he greeted me with warmth. Would you believe, Mr Reigate was tall, aristocratic in bearing, wore a tweed suit and moustache, smoked a pipe and spoke, as I would eventually discover, with a formidable Public School accent. Here was my perfect embodiment of the Upper Class Englishman! Later that day, he drove me home and on the way, pointed out the sights. Home was Turner's Close, Wildwood Road, on Hampstead Heath. Not even in my dreams had I entered such a house in such surroundings! Mrs Patricia Tama Reigate met me at the door. A pretty, dark-haired Jewish woman, she had, daringly for that time, married the Gentile Mr Reigate. She settled me into a beautiful room on the top floor, with a sloping ceiling and a lovely view over the garden and the Heath. This was where I would spend the first few months of my stay in England.

Chapter 18

MAY/JUNE 1939. Even an innocent like me can see that war is imminent and I am very worried about my mother who, except for Uncle Jack and family, is now totally alone in Milan. From her frequent letters I gather that my brother's trial is impending, and finally, that she has managed to secure a brave Italian lawyer to defend him. Although it seems incredible, what really and truly had started out as not much more than a schoolboy adventure looks likely to get him the death sentence or certainly a very long time in jail.

Another letter reaches me from Mother. The sentence has been handed down: incredibly, thirty years in prison! My twenty-one-year-old brother has escaped the death penalty by a whisker, his defence being just as good as it was allowed to be. Thirty nightmare years! The lawyer was simply only allowed to plead for mercy. The girl-friend's evidence, the copies of his writings and mine, the mutilated passport, all have been totally damning.

Thirty years! Remissions for good conduct unheard of. Most of his life over! And political jails in Italy are notorious. Opponents of the Régime can expect no mercy. This was the country where they fed litres of castor oil to resisters during and after the March on Rome. The trial had been held in camera, so Mother had not been allowed to attend. The girl too had received a jail-sentence but I do not know for how long. Such a terrible waste! And for my mother, what a tragedy.

She was making frantic efforts to get to see John, who had been moved to the political fortress prison on Elba. Sure enough, after an unexplained silence from her came news that she had been to Elba and contrived permission to visit John. She had made this trip alone from Milan with not enough money to cover her expenses, But she managed it! She sold the remaining rings from her fingers to pay her expenses as she went along, including her lonely crossing to Elba and for bribes where necessary. Alone and on foot, she carried parcels of food and other comforts up the hill to the penitentiary, and was then kept waiting for hours. When she finally was allowed to see her son, she found he was being kept in solitary confinement, in chains. It is still at times too painful to think about.

Facing the fact that there is absolutely nothing to be done now for John, there is one other objective left: getting Mother to the UK. I know that if war breaks out she will never get here. It is a fortunate coincidence that Mrs Reigate, who I think wants me out of her hair during the day (perhaps my stay is not quite the success everyone had hoped) has secured a job for me at Bloomsbury House. This committee for Jewish Refugees does the preliminary work on behalf of the Home Office in processing immigration applications. Once again, I am errand boy and filing clerk, Whenever Mother's papers come into my hands, I make sure, somewhat improperly, that they go to the top of the pile, thus saving months of painstaking procedure and delay.

Chapter 19

MY WORK AT BLOOMSBURY HOUSE is quite happy and I am learning English at a reasonable speed, although I make a lot of gaffes which amuse most people but irritate Mrs Reigate. Once when she saw me scratching myself, she asked why I was doing it: innocently, I said, "Instinct," and she promptly compared me to a monkey.

Anyway I have decided not to restart school: yet another country, yet another start from the bottom seems just too much. I have lived to regret that decision for the whole rest of my life. Who was there for advice? So I continue with my job and resume my Paris practice of wandering around the city when I can. I contact my few friends and relations in London: in particular my very beautiful young Aunt Henni, Mother's half-sister who lives in Seven Sisters Road. She is very kind to me, but of course has her own life to live. After all, she is just six years older than I am. She is still straining every sinew to get my Grandfather Süssman and all the family over from Germany. In fact her younger brother Horst (later Shaul) and younger sister Lore emigrate direct to Palestine during 1939 thanks to Kindertransports, and her parents and other sister Fella make it to Nottingham one at a time during the same year.

As I have hinted, my relationship with Mrs Reigate is not too successful. I just cannot seem to live up to her expectations. Mr Reigate however is quite kind and even takes me on business outings in his car. Thus, one day, in his convertible, he takes me to Leicester, which he pronounces Lestah. A pleasant memory indeed and my first visit to a provincial English town.

The Reigates employ a young German/Jewish nanny for their three year old daughter and she offers me considerable solace when I feel lonely and miserable and I often do the same for her. Sadly, I cannot even remember her name. This Reigate period does enable me to broaden my reading. From a wonderful library in their attic, I remember in particular deriving immense joy from *Lettres de Mon Moulin* by Alphonse Daudet and *Les Miserables* by Victor Hugo and *The Three Musketeers* and *The Count of Monte Cristo* by Alexandre Dumas. What with the *Beau Geste* stories by P.C. Wren, I am developing a very catholic reading taste indeed. Sabatini's *Torquemada and the Spanish Inquisition* I find fascinating and very educational. Hitler certainly did not invent religious persecution!

Great news! Today at Bloomsbury House I hear that Mother has been granted an immigration permit. This will still take some time to go through. I pray there will be no war to prevent her coming. I notify Mother of the impending permit (because of my occupation I know before anyone else) and she starts preparations at her end. Once again, the most pressing problem is a transit visa through France, but she cannot even apply until the English visa arrives. In the meantime, I keep working away at my job where thrillingly I am presented to the Vice Empress of India, Lady Reading, who gives me ten shillings. It seems she is Jewish and a great supporter of Bloomsbury House.

Suddenly, out of the blue, Mrs Reigate informs me that I am to meet a Berkshire poultry farmer and his wife, with a view to living and working with them. She takes me for an interview in deepest Berkshire, in beautiful countryside near Streatley and Goring-on-Thames, and I am accepted. I am to start shortly and meantime I return to London to pack.

Chapter 20

PERHAPS IT WAS MY UNTIDINESS, perhaps neglect of my gardening chores, perhaps "my instincts", perhaps I just didn't live up to the Reigate's expectations, perhaps ... who knows? ... Anyway, the Reigate era was ending. London had been good. Life had been good. The weather had been good. I had begun to enjoy watching Sunday cricket on the Heath and observing what I thought to be the upper-class lifestyle of the English. I had treasured the time spent admiring the wonderful buildings and Art Galleries and so, with not too many regrets and armed with a still very moderate knowledge of English, very few clothes and even less money, I arrived at White Hayes Farm to live with and work for Mr and Mrs Frank Hundleby.

Before I go on, I must record my enormous gratitude to the Reigates, for despite the slight blips, they had been good to me and had brought me to Britain. Without them, who knows? I tried to visit them in later years, but they were no longer in Turner's Close. My efforts to trace them failed, but in 1945 or '46, while in the Army, I read in the papers that a British diplomat attached to the Embassy in Budapest had been thrown out of a car at high speed in some accident or attack. The diplomat's name was Patricia Tama Reigate. I did not receive the impression that the accident had been fatal and on my next leave made efforts to trace her or her husband, but again to no avail. It has left quite a gap.

To come back to August 1939 and the Hundlebys: Frank (not that I was ever encouraged to call him that) was a handsome man with blond hair and a high degree of intelligence and strong white teeth that always clenched a pipe. Alas, no moustache! Mrs H. was a bony flat-chested lady whose priorities were her husband and the farm with its sixteen hilly acres and seemingly endless thousands of chickens. Tuberculin tested, of course! Through no fault of my new employer's, settling in proved to be somewhat difficult. I hadn't heard from Mother, had not yet seen Celia in Nottingham and of course there was no news of John. I felt isolated. The work was extremely hard but healthy and I was treated well. I received the princely salary of two shillings and sixpence a week, plus board. Out of that income, a newly acquired smoking habit encouraged by Mr Hundleby had to be supported and I even managed to buy necessities such as long-johns, shirts and stamps. I was always being accused jokingly of eating like a horse and indeed the food was plentiful and good, so I did my best to live up to my equine reputation. As the workload was truly enormous, I could also claim to work like a horse.

Mother's silence continued and I was getting frantic. To make my panic worse, on the third of September, we heard on the wireless Chamberlain's famous speech declaring war on Germany. This was World War Two! Now I knew with absolute certainty that my mother would never get to Britain, as any pre-war entry permit would be invalidated. So I cried. Not because of the war, but because of my mother. The Hundlebys laughed at me for crying but their mothers were not stuck in enemy country.

Then, a very few days later, there was a phone call from Mother! She was in London! Miraculously, she had done it again. Now she was on her way to Nottingham to stay with her sister Gina and family. Without entry visa, she had travelled to France and there presented her English entry permit. The authorities for once showed humanity and permitted my mother to travel solo through a France already at war. She then presented herself in Harwich where she was detained overnight by Immigration, as her visa had been invalidated by the outbreak of war. But what could they have done with her? As she would have said, with her arms spread wide, "What can a woman do?" So the Home Office relented and she made her determined entry into England. She told me later that Jack and Sally and their daughters Margot and Elena were still in Italy, fearfully expecting imminent internment. Dispossession and internment were the twin threats held over all Jewish residents who had not yet left the country as ordered by the Italian Government's antisemitic proclamations. It would be many years before I heard from any of them again and in the case of Uncle Jack, never.

In Streatley, things went on at an even pace. Every Tuesday we made an outing to Reading, the biggest nearby town, in the Hundlebys' little jalopy. We bought the weekly supplies and lunched at Lyon's Corner House with wonderful, mouth-watering regularity. Those steak and kidney puddings! Sixpence each, served at table by waitresses in black uniforms and white frilly caps and aprons. The epitome of luxury. Then an hour's slow drive back to Streatley and hard work. Farms are no respecters of Saturdays and Sundays, so the Tuesday excursion was the only break, Working hours went with daylight and sometimes beyond.

Chickens are filthy things to work with. I detested them, yet I had to carry 1 cwt. bags of chicken-feed to them on my back, up and down those sixteen hilly acres. And believe me, that was no chicken-feed! My muscles were building muscles. And this, despite the fact that we had a pony and cart. I have to record that the pony was called Sausage and that it was subjected to marginally less weight-carrying than I was.

Having discovered that I could augment my income by poaching pheasant which had strayed from Lord Iliffe's adjoining estate, I pursued this enterprise with admirable zeal and flogged the birds for half a crown a time to the Reading shops. Sorry, Lord Iliffe! But what a lovely feeling to have those luxurious silver half-crown coins jingling in my pocket!

One memory I relate with some reluctance, but with total candour since this tale is all about making a clean breast of things, Farmer

Hundleby had bought fifteen young cockerels of the very best strain to fertilise the hens. They were his pride and joy. Their value to him was increased by the fact that it was a kind of miracle to obtain these rare birds in wartime. Having been instructed by the farmer to move these priceless princes of their breed from one compound to another, I properly carried them hanging by their feet, two to each hand, as was the recognised mode of transportation. So, imagine my horror when I found that one of the birds had become lame in transit! I was mortally afraid of Hundleby's reaction on discovering the damage. In a blind panic, certain that I would at least meet the same fate as the cockerel, I decided to do away with the offending bird altogether. At that stage of my poultry-farming career, I had not yet learned how to wring a chicken's neck in the recognised fashion, so instead, I thumped it several times over the head with a hammer, Leaving my victim for dead in an upturned water bucket hidden in a shed, I went back to the house.

But conscience doth make cowards of us all. That night, I could barely sleep. Remorse was killing me. When I did manage to fall asleep, I had terrible nightmares, during which I heard that damned cock crow and crow, and crow. In the morning, I rushed down to dispose of the body and found the water bucket overturned. The cockerel was still alive! He was fluttering feebly on the floor and I had to administer the *coup de grâce*. Murderer me! I buried the bird under the roots of a tree and walked away with my conscience for companion. During the following days Mr Hundleby kept counting his little flock and, hardly surprisingly, he always came up one short. And I kept wishing he would for God's sake give up. Well, you've read how one crime leads to another: one of the cursed farm dogs kept sniffing round that burial tree and I was ready to despatch him too, to cover up my sin. At night, I continued to have awful dreams which always culminated in my being a murderer and burying human bodies, mostly in disused windmills. You see how the crime had grown. I an relieved that the police never became aware of my homicidal dreams which went on for years.

Well, I was never discovered and the dog finally gave up sniffing around and for a while life returned to normal. I corresponded with Mother and with cousin Joe in Nottingham and of course, Celia. We listened to the wireless and followed the non-progress of the Phoney War. We heard of a rabbit being killed by a German air raid near the Forth Bridge and we laughed heartily and we sang "Run Rabbit, Run Rabbit, Run Run Run.' All very jolly then. But the jolliness and cheer did not last much longer.

In the late autumn, the farmer informed me that he was highly pleased with my work and that he was giving me a rise! The labourer is worthy of his hire. Henceforth, I would earn £1 per week. Oh riches, oh splendour! Unheard-of wealth! What could I not do with a whole pound? But then, the crushing blow: fifteen shillings would be deducted for board. Now I had to be rich on five shillings. Kind though they were to me in other ways, the Hundlebys certainly made me understand what cheap labour meant. This sort of situation was being multiplied a thousand times throughout Britain.

The winter moved in very suddenly, just about the fiercest on record. Everything was cocooned in ice, including me, and each blade of grass was a separate icicle pointing upwards, but the chickens still had to be fed. That's when the farmer caught the 'flu. His wife looked after him. I looked after the chickens. Then the farmer got better, his wife caught the 'flu, and he looked after her. And I still looked after the chickens. Then I became ill (I had always had nasal trouble). But still I helped to look after the damned chickens. Mother put an end to the whole situation. Under the pretext of her own ill health, she called me urgently to Nottingham and I joined the family for the very first time in this country.

Chapter 21

MOST IMMIGRANTS, refugees, settlers, incomers, call them what you will, tended to congregate around previous arrivals in the major towns. Thus relatives. friends and business contacts became focal points for the new arrivals who clustered around them and could often become a real burden. They actually moved in with their very generous and long suffering hosts for indefinite periods, or looked to them for material support and constant advice. Since the newest incomers were mostly in dire straits, they assumed that a certain amount of help was their due, particularly as the earlier arrivals were seemingly already settled and enjoying a better lifestyle. This partial illusion was caused by the fact that some of the early arrivers had managed to acquire a small house or start a little business and that did seem riches indeed. So the hosts, who had enough trouble looking after their own, now found themselves with other sets of dependants on their hands. In many cases, they responded nobly and this was certainly so with my Uncle Victor and Auntie Gina who, having put down roots in Nottingham with their sons Joe and Manfred, were not without their own difficulties. They were just beginning to find their feet when my maternal grandparents, Süssman and Betty and daughter Fella arrived from Leipzig and settled very near to them. Victor's comfortable semi-detached at 2B Ramsdale Crescent which housed most of us at one time or another, had a long, steep back-garden with a latch-gate at the top. Just facing it across the road was 102 Winchester Street where my newly-arrived grandparents Rotenstein settled. I feel sure that Victor assumed, at least in part, the burden of that responsibility. How I wish now that I had been mature enough at that time to thank Victor and Gina for what they did for all the family over those years. A lot of things were taken for granted.

Of the other Rotenstein children, Lore and Horst, as previously mentioned, had settled in Palestine. Henni was still working in London, carving out a career for herself. My grandfather had given up work. He was a rather squat, portly gentleman, with the most handsome mass of wavy, silvery hair. He, my step-grandmother Betty whom we called Oma and Fella, their eldest daughter, all lived together. Fella was a plump young woman who was to remain the only unmarried member of the family but in later years became a fairy godmother to many of Henni's progeny. Henni herself was tragically killed in a motorway smash. Historically, there was no love lost between Oma on the one side and Mother and Auntie Gina on the other, but that did improve over the years.

About Victor and Gina: he was a most imposing figure of a man, with deportment to match. She was unchanged from the German days: busy, bustling, kind, but always with a little worried frown on her face. Everyone's mum. So it seemed only natural that Mother move in with them for a while and it followed that she called me there too, never to return to Berkshire. Despite the Hundlebys' general kindness, the £1 per week (less board) and their interchangeable 'flu bouts held little appeal for me. So: end of career amongst my feathered friends.

I did not actually go to the Dessaus, but temporarily joined my sister Celia at the house of her employers, the Saunders. Mother followed shortly after. In that sprawling, ancient house, with its very real medal-rattling ghost, we were welcome guests and for the short time we stayed, were made very comfortable. Indeed, the family ghost also did his best to make us feel at home, or at least to provide light entertainment; although I considered his idea of light entertainment to be just a little too blood-chilling for my taste. In that ancient, creaky house it was easy to hear ghostly footsteps and this was a fairly frequent event. We scarcely took any notice, but one night the whole thing just went beyond a joke. In the large, cavernous living room where Celia and I sat doing a stint of baby-sitting, there was a glass cabinet mounted to the wall above the fireplace. This contained impressive rows of medals won in some forgotten war by the original Colonel Saunders who had built this house. The cabinet was always carefully secured by mortice lock. So, there we sat, Celia and I, listening very quietly to the wireless (no TV in those days) when suddenly we heard quite distinct heavy footsteps clomping down a long corridor towards the room in which we sat. The door opened and the footsteps passed directly by us, actually stirring up a breeze. They then proceeded the remaining few paces to the medal cabinet, the doors of which swung outward quite slowly. The medals began to rattle in some kind of frenzied St Vitus dance. We two sat there absolutely transfixed. We had both turned white and I am positive that my hair literally stood on end. After a moment, Celia grabbed my hand and together we listened to the departing footfall of our terrifying visitor. Creaking loudly, a door opened on the far side of the room, without any apparent help. The sound of receding footsteps concluded the unwelcome but seemingly very real visit. I was sixteen at the time and Celia twenty and we were certainly much too young and cynical to be disposed to believe in anything supernatural. For both of us to experience the same happening, it really had to be true! Mr Saunders was only mildly surprised when we jabbered on about our shocking visitation on his return home.

I recall Joe Saunders as a businessman, with the very upright bearing of the Regular Army Officer; understandable, since he was a direct descendant of the founder of the Sherwood Foresters Regiment whose spirit had caused us such palpitations. He was friendly with Uncle Victor; hence his sponsorship to bring Celia from Italy to a job in their household and our invitation to stay there until we got organised. His wife Bo was pink, fluffy and very plump and they had two little daughters. She took very seriously her responsibilities towards the Jews of Europe: this included patiently correcting my English and, most important, teaching me how to eat kippers. For someone who had never seen kippers before, this was quite an achievement.

Next came the problem of a job. Now sixteen, I had to find means of supporting Mother and myself. She was totally convinced that a Jewish boy absolutely must have a trade or a profession so that, when an advert appeared in the *Nottingham Evening Post* looking for an engineering apprentice, Mother positively knew it had to be intended just for me. I duly applied and I did obtain an interview and out of twenty-odd applicants, I was the one who was offered the job! As Mother had absolutely known: the Lord was providing. In view of my aforementioned non-existent technical skills and only moderate English, my selection savoured of the improbable and ridiculous.

(Author's note: In sports as in matters practical and mechanical, I always had two left hands and two left feet. Switching on an electric light all by myself, wholly unaided, I considered a major success and still do. Thus, it was clear that this particular ambition of my mother's on my behalf was suffused with the roseate glow of optimism.)

The simple and somewhat pitiful explanation emerged when, bright and shiny, I reported to the manager on the first morning. He called me into his office and bade me sit beside him, on his side of the desk. There he produced a well-thumbed glossy photographic publication, featuring some highly interesting exotic pictures. At the same time he rested his hand, in friendly fashion, lightly on my thigh. This brought to an abrupt and instant end my budding engineering career! I never even got as far as the work-shop floor. For the time being the Lord had stopped providing, at least according to Mother's requirements. At this point perhaps, I should explain with no false modesty that I was a nice looking boy and in those days often experienced interested reaction from both sexes, but I was well able to distinguish between welcome overtures and others and this one definitely came under the heading of "others".

Once again, the question of career had to be dealt with. We did not wish to be a continuing burden on the Saunders or the Dessaus. Happily, as ever, Mother knew someone. Mr Charles Noskovitch, a friend of my father's back in the Chemnitz days, was the owner of a flourishing stocking factory in Ilkeston, some seven miles from Nottingham. By now his name had become Noskwith and he was the first "tycoon" I had ever met. Over tea with Mother at his home, he agreed to employ me as an apprentice stocking machine operator. The poor misguided fool! I am sure I held back the development of Charnos Hosiery Ltd. (now a very large public company) by quite some time.

I took digs in Ilkeston within yards of the factory. There I learned to eat bangers and mash drowned in gravy and was very kindly treated by the family who had taken me in to share a room with another lodger called Schofield.

I was apprenticed to one Jim Rawlinson. He was a nineteen-year-old swaggering muscle-bound ape who didn't know what to make of me, this alien from outer space. I do believe that he, in common with most of Ilkeston, had never seen a foreigner before. And with such a strange accent yet! But at least the girls, in and out of the factory, were overwhelmingly in favour. Here, the slight language problem was no obstacle at all. We managed just fine. Well, "you know what mill-girls are!" In the canteen and outside work, a whole new world was opening up for me. My education was certainly broadening and not necessarily just in English! One of my willing teachers was Nora. Twenty-four years old to my seventeen, she took me to the cinema and for walks in the country. If I did not respond to her the way she had hoped, I can only blame my immaturity. Nora, if you're still around, a lively octogenarian, please forgive me for being such a wet fish!

Jim, my "mate", was a bully. He gave me a very hard time, but he did show me the realities of working in a factory. He tyrannised me into becoming a machinist. Thus I was soon promoted to working my own machine which knitted heels onto the fully-fashioned stockings. Here I had an assistant, Elsie, a voluptuous female in her thirties. I think a large part of her livelihood came from extra-curricular activities. She had breasts like mountains and a mouth like the valley that separated them. Because we were on piece-work, I could never work fast enough for her. Her wages depended on my speed, and well, I wasn't exactly the fastest or the greatest machinist under pressure. She was constantly screaming at me. So one day, trying to keep up with her, I had an accident with my machine. It was a calamity. We were out of action for some time. This drew upon me the further wrath of my assistant, colourfully expressed, and Mr Noskwith himself issued some stern warnings.

Just as I was strange to most of my fellow workers, they and their customs were new and strange to me. They spoke with an accent you could stir with a stick. They ate "cobs" and "mashed" their tea. Unlike the women, the men tended to be suspicious of anything alien and one had to be careful of what one said. Indeed, I got into quite serious trouble because in all innocence, I showed some of my "Balilla" photographs to fellow workers. Within days, I was called to the police station and thoroughly cross-examined. For some time thereafter my movements were restricted. Although I was a "friendly alien" I was compelled to report to the police for permission before I undertook any journey, no matter how short. This even included trips to Nottingham.

I suppose I was lucky. The conflict had suddenly erupted for real in France after the long Phoney War. One result was a tremendous security panic and indiscriminate arrests and internment. As a friendly alien, I just escaped this, but so-called enemy aliens (and that included all German Jews) were rounded up indiscriminately and sent to camps on the Isle of Man and Canada and Australia. Being Poles, all my family escaped this very ironic and unjust predicament. It is a fact that the Intelligence Officers and police who handled these internments were convinced that the internees, nearly all Jews, were the "Enemy within the Gates", the Fifth Column. They genuinely thought that if Hitler came, they themselves would be inside the wire and we Jews on the outside guarding them for the Führer!

About this time Mother joined me in Ilkeston and Manfred became an occasional visitor. We had taken digs with a family called Gamble. Fred, about ten years my senior, became my mentor. Despite his heavily pomaded "short back and sides", he was very wise in the ways of his world. It was he who first took me to pubs and boxing matches and introduced me to many minor champion fighters of the time. In the pubs, he only allowed me shandy and taught me to drink slowly and sociably. He showed me how to get along with my peers and with barmaids and protected me from the xenophobes who abounded in that time and place.

I had reached the heady heights of three pounds fifteen shillings per week average earnings, and gave it all to my mother, except for pocket money of about half a crown or a little more, depending on the piece-work results. On this I managed to travel to Nottingham by bus on some weekends (with police permission) to stay with the Dessaus. I even managed to take out a girl or two, particularly one Pauline Hallam, rosy-skinned and gorgeous, and this despite the competition from all those uniformed heroes home on leave who thronged the dance halls. The girls, some also in uniform, came from a background very different to my Ilkeston environment. They were "middle class" and "brought up proper". Socially, it was an agreeable Jekyll and Hyde existence.

The girls in Ilkeston took me for walks in the fields, and the girls in Nottingham took me to Socials, where they taught me to dance to a selection of lovely memorable tunes such as "Stardust", "I'll See You In My Dreams", "You Were Never Lovelier", "Blue Moon", "I'll Be Seeing You" and so many others, particularly those patriotic British songs. We smooched to the big-band sounds of Glenn Miller and Joe Loss and Tommy Dorsey, and crooners such as Frank Sinatra, Bing Crosby, Vera Lynn and Anne Shelton. The music's ended, but the melody lingers on . . . My mentor and companion on most of those occasions was cousin Joe. Owing to petrol rationing, necking could seldom happen in the backs of cars, so the back rows of cinemas and draughty doorways were the frustrating venues in my quest for the golden goal. Condoms were only just coming to the fore, but they were mainly called French Letters and "nice" girls did not allude to them, although we whispered many daring jokes about them in the men's lavatories. Oh youth of today! You don't know how lucky you are!

Jim Rawlinson had been a-courting a twenty-three-year old girl called Norma. One day, he burst into the factory with the news that he and Norma were getting married. I was as much surprised as honoured when he invited me to be his best man/usher. Over the next weeks he explained my duties to me. The great day dawned. Punctually we arrived in church: she, in her wartime austerity bridal gown and he in his Sunday-go-to-church suit, flower in lapel. At the pulpit I duly handed over the ring and raced down the aisle at the end of the Service to take up my position as usher, beside the door of the wedding car. I was sweating with the tension and responsibility of the moment. When the happy couple, as yet unaware of impending disaster, came out of church, I opened the car door with a gallant flourish. Jim handed in his bride, oh-so-gently. He followed. He sat down. Hand on door jamb, he leaned forward to give me some last instructions. At that instant, proudly collaborative, I slammed the door firmly shut . . . onto his fingers!! An almighty roar burst from his throat. Then came a frozen silence, followed in turn by the most colourful and varied stream of swear-words that anyone could ever imagine. And never once did he repeat himself! The blushing bride blushed even more, while I was busy trying to wrench open the door and release Jim's mangled hand. Picture the scene! I still do . . . My last view of the happy couple was of the hired car departing at breakneck speed towards hospital instead of the dream honeymoon. When they returned a week or so later, his arm was still in a sling and I was not flavour of the month. It was one of the more embarrassing and, dare I say, painful moments of my life. It still hurts me to think about it. Particularly when I laugh . . .

In concluding the Charnos Chapter of my career, I regret having to recall that I wrecked my machine once more and was lucky that Mr Noskwith did not wreck me! He did, however, bid me an urgent and not too fond farewell.

Chapter 22

IT IS 1940, the year of the German advance through Belgium and Holland into France. The corrupt and inefficient French High Command offers little to stop the Germans and our own expeditionary forces have to be evacuated through Dunkirk. The German Luftwaffe has started to bomb England and the nation is beginning to experience total war. At this time, Mother is taken to hospital in Nottingham for a major operation. She has a large growth in her womb. While she is away, Celia, who has been living away from us for some time, comes to stay with me. That is when we experience our first real live bombing raid. Owing to the presence of a large steel works on the outskirts of Ilkeston, the Germans have decided to pay us a visit. Those of you who are in my age group will perhaps not require a replay of the sensations we experienced when we first had to suffer an air attack and others will have seen films on the subject, but even they cannot possibly feel the bowel-loosening terror when living through one's first raid. Those terrifying sirens were the overture, followed by the drone of the bombers' engines and the noise of the anti-aircraft guns. Then the whistle and crash of the bombs. This particular bombardment was short but very fierce. We were both thrown violently out of our beds and very badly shaken. The building was damaged. We were scared out of our minds! Of course we had been told always to take shelter, but who listens, until it is too late. Those sirens: I am not sure that they were not the worst part of it. The howling sound penetrated your sleep and was a terrifying warning that you were a sitting duck and were quite likely to be killed without any chance of defending yourself. Then that cacophony of ear-splitting sound caused by combined ack-ack guns and aircraft engines and bombs falling all around. A very good scenario for a man-made hell. Well, I suppose if you did not first die of fear or enemy bombs, it must have helped to mould your character.

One regular visitor who braved the unpleasant wartime travelling conditions was my young cousin Manfred. He came to see us quite frequently, mainly, I think, in the hope of collecting the most recent jokes from me to take back to school. He actually took notes!

The need for a job dictated a return to Nottingham and in the fullness of time, Mother and I took up lodgings in Lenton Boulevard at the home of an octogenarian solo-playing fiend, Mrs Kilmister. She was a lovely little Victorian lady in lovely little Victorian clothes in her lovely little semi-detached Victorian house, but when she played solo for ha'penny stakes, she became a holy terror!

Just next to our house there was a temporary wartime emergency ambulance station. Amongst the daredevil drivers working there was a Jewish girl called Jean Morris. I had a tremendous crush on her and indeed she was very fond of me, as she might have been of her favourite dog or cat, This girl, who had everything, was killed in a car crash some time later.

I do not propose to litter this tale with precise details of my subsequent employments. They were not many and not interesting, but later that year I found myself working for a very smooth, handsome older man of twenty-four called Harold Fainlight. He and his two associates were employing Mother as secretary and of course she managed to tell them I was the man they were looking for. Harold Fainlight was opening a factory engaged in precision engraving and he wanted me to take charge of it. The "factory" consisted of two pantograph machines and this time I actually did learn to work them properly.

Our government sub-contracts for precision instruments kept us working really hard and at our busiest, we operated two shifts of two men each, including myself. For a reason that escapes me, Harold Fainlight and his associates decided to move their various activities to London. That included me, so we all packed our bags and like proper camp followers, moved to London. We took a nice flat in Camden Town on Camden Road, overlooking the Regent Canal, The building is still there. It is called Highstone Mansions and the rent was £2 per week. This included the Canal View and the Canal Smell. Mother kept house and I went back to work.

We opened a small factory/office in Poland Street, of which I was manager and general factotum. In the building next door, Mr Fainlight and his partners had started a wholesale and manufacturing fancy-goods business. My duties on the engraving side consisted of obtaining contracts by calling on factories engaged in war work, running the engraving and also helping in the warehouse. And all the time the bombs were dropping all around.

During 1941, 1942 and 1943, I continued to do the same job. I had a great friend and co-worker called Len Cartwright and together we scoured London for any available talent. I have since learned that he died about ten years ago in Skegness, where his wife who was a gipsy read palms, and he stood outside taking photos. We went to dances in places like the People's Palace in the East End and some obscure dance hall near Clapham Common. I learned to knock back pints of beer, which was pretty gruesome in its wartime flavouring and I was not above getting stupidly drunk at times. There was one occasion when I went dancing in my first-ever brand new suit, made to measure at Fifty Shilling Tailors, at the expense of the pooled family clothing coupons. That night, I got very drunk and at one point actually had to rush out of the dance hall for fresh air. I absolutely felt the urgent need to sit down somewhere, so I chose the edge of the pavement, but first, I meticulously and carefully removed and folded my new jacket, placed it carefully on the filthy ground to protect my new trousers, then solemnly sat down on it!

That period in London basically consisted of the four B's: Bombs, Booze, Birds and Boredom. The bombs were beginning to ease off, the beer did not agree with me, the birds preferred men in uniform and the boredom was the sum total of all those.

In Nottingham, I had joined the Home Guard. Of course, everyone has heard about Dad's Army, but really the London Unit to which I was transferred from Nottingham consisted mainly of younger men. We were issued with gas masks and the smart uniforms of the private soldier, but of guns we had none. That is, until we were trained to help in the manning of ack-ack guns on Hampstead Heath. A first taste of active service! The night duty was spectacular: overhead the drone of German aircraft and the dramatic criss-crossing of the searchlights, the thump thump of our guns and the crashing of the bombs somewhere over London, No time for fear: we were just young and stupid. I must have distinguished myself as usual, because I stayed firmly rooted as a private during my entire Home Guard service.

I suppose that my work on precision engraving would have ex-empted me from military Service but thanks anyway to the suspicious attitude towards foreigners that still befuddled the minds of the British government, I could neither be called up to, nor volunteer for, the British Army. In common with many others, like my cousin Joe back in Nottingham, I was longing to join the war. At about this time, the Polish Government-in-Exile decided to call up all Poles of military age then residing in Britain. The option, the Poles said, was to be posted as deserters by them and thus to be rendered liable for call-up to the British colours. As one man, all Polish Jews declined the honour of joining the Polish Army and thus happily awaited their summons to take the Queen's Shilling. I confess that had any other country but Germany invaded Poland in 1939, I would have wished them the best of luck. Even in exile in Britain, they were still mouthing their foul racist sentiments. (Clearly, this was not always the case.) So the British hierarchy's change of attitude towards us was warmly welcomed by all.

For some reason I do not quite recall, I did not join up from London, but from Nottingham, together with Cousin Joe. Then back to work in London to await my summons. Young fools that we were! Dying to go into the Army, forgive the pun ...

Life in the capital proceeded as normal, if you could call that normal. I had a fiery romance with an attractive barmaid called Bobby who worked in a pub called the Green Man in Berwick Street. She faithfully promised to kill herself if I were ever called up. Instead, she deluged me with adoring letters. I wish I had kept them. What cosy fireside reading they would still make! Another lady of the time was the secretary at the warehouse where I worked. Her name was Molly. She was pretty and married and lonely, and willing to bestow the benefit of her greater experience upon this humble youth.

It was, to use a more modern expression, quite hairy to escort a girl home at night. There was always the danger of air-raids and absolutely no certainty that the Tube would not get stuck somewhere in the tunnels. And of course, the husband just might turn up! Getting back to my own home was equally hazardous. On top of that, all underground stations were packed with masses of humanity sheltering from air-raids. You tiptoed your way around and over the recumbent bodies, through the smell of thousands of people packed so tightly together. I don't suppose anyone who lived through that time could ever forget those stations and those masses of people and the amazing atmosphere that prevailed. Mostly, the crowd sheltering consisted of older men, women and children and their spirits appeared incredibly high. Often there was music and singing and you were welcome to join in. Such incredibly high morale and bravery, despite the suffering and the privations. Then, you walked the streets in daylight and saw what was left of their homes, what remained for them to see when they emerged from those tunnels. Rows and rows of houses that had been there the night before were gone or largely demolished. There was the grotesque view of entire walls of tenements having been blasted away, exposing the remains of the apartments totally open to one's horrified gaze. Furniture still in place, just as if the inhabitants were yet sitting or cooking or sleeping there, but no walls. Broken doll's houses.

Two of the three partners for whom I worked, not including Harold Fainlight, managed to get themselves into trouble with the authorities. I think the offence was connected somehow with the black market which at that time was everyone's favourite hobby. The two gentlemen were brought to trial and I was called as a witness. I was supposed to know about the movement of certain goods from the warehouse, but truly had no idea. I recalled my younger days in Italy and my fear of officialdom, so that even the thought of going into a witness box surrounded by bewigged and begowned lawyers and officials and policemen filled me with fear and foreboding. I wish I could say that on the appointed day the fear just vanished and that I stepped into the witness box ice-cool and debonair, top-hat, white tie and tails. In the event, I was trembling and white faced and must have appeared a greater liar than the two men on trial. When one of the lawyers suggested that my testimony was a "tissue of lies", I did not even know what it meant. I really had tried to tell the truth, but my appearance must have created a terrible impression. I wonder if my testimony helped him on his way. As it turned out, I never saw the gentleman again.

Shortly afterwards, I was called for my medical which I passed A1 all too easily and in December 1943, I was instructed to report to the Royal West Kent Regiment, Invicta Lines, Maidstone. At last, at last, at the age of nineteen, I had become a soldier in the British Army! Hitler and Mussolini, tremble!

Book 5
The Army

Chapter 23

A Time for Reflection

WHEN WRITING a mainly factual story such as this, style tends to become subordinated to the need to relate events as simply as possible. The well-chosen word, the neatly turned phrase, the use of language that turns it all into a shapely form, like a nicely rounded calf or ankle, this all tends to be forgotten. You feel that on occasion there should be a little pull at the heart-strings, thanks at least in part to the virtuosity of your phrasing, but this does not come easily. For instance, I want to describe my mother to you, really describe her, the woman and not just her vital statistics. But how do you present such an extraordinary person? When our wandering years began, she was certainly quite a pampered lady. The times that followed, the ever-lowering and narrowing spiral in the standard of her expectations, must have taken an enormous amount of mental and physical adjustment. She was a lovely woman of great strength of character, the seed of which grew in adversity and really only flowered when she was forced to take charge of her own destiny. Not only strength, but hidden abilities came to the surface. She became adept at handling people and developed her remarkable talent for languages. By the time we left Germany, she already spoke and wrote German, Polish, Russian and Yiddish; this last, a most unusual accomplishment, in which she could even take dictation in her fashion. As a shorthand-typist, she was outstanding. And then, in her middle years, owing to our travels, she added fluent French, Italian and English to her list of linguistic achievements. She was extremely bright, perhaps not always very tolerant, but passionately devoted to us children. She made friends easily and kept those friendships for many years, despite our migrations.

As for us, well, we were wrapped up in the warm mantle of her love. She fought like a tiger for our well-being and indeed she often had to. Sometimes that meant that everyday necessities such as food and rent might have had to take precedence over what were to her our trivial needs for swimming lessons, sports equipment, bicycles, toys and such. Just so long as you did well in school! In that connection, if she felt that your marks were not up to standard, she was quite capable of waging war with the teachers. She had strict codes of behaviour. Lying and deceit were anathema to her. I was caught out several times and always punished. Once, when I was fourteen or so, I told her I was going to meet a school-friend after supper. Instead, she caught me in the street in the company of a pretty older girl and she gave me a stinging wallop in the face in front of her. Thus she at once reminded me of her views on lying and of the child I still was.

Through these pages you have seen me grow up. The years had taught me about myself and that hard world outside. I had probably become fairly streetwise, but never managed to grow a tough outer skin. I suppose my early encounters with persecution, illness and death, as well as the frequent interrogations and occasional imprisonments, had made me distrustful and rather fearful of outside influences. But the time had finally come to make my own way in this world and thus, in December of 1943 I found myself on a platform at Nottingham Station on a freezing wet, miserable morning ready to embark on the Great Adventure in the company of my cousin Joe. There must have been another dozen or so embryonic heroes on that platform taking leave of mothers and girlfriends quietly, with perhaps the odd tear, but with dignity and lots of stiff upper lip. Now, turn your glance towards Joe and me, going to War! Surrounded by uncounted well-wishers consisting of a selection of grandmothers, mothers, aunties, brothers, sisters, cousins, friends and an odd girlfriend or two, we were surely setting out to win the war within the next week and all by ourselves! Lots of hankies on display and much weeping and wailing and gnashing of teeth. A Jewish melodrama was being enacted and decorum was not going to stand in its way.

With much relief, Joe and I at last boarded the train, waved one last heroes' farewell, and steamed off to our brave new life, leaving behind a legion of heartbroken girls, or so we flattered ourselves. Certainly, when we had been together in Nottingham, we had tried to paint the town red. My cousin Manfred was left out of all this, because he was deemed too young for us. What a difference three years make at that age! Really, he was the clever one. He never did get called up to the Army and successfully stepped into our shoes on the Nottingham Home Front. Lest I create the belief that we were only interested in girls, let me please add that Joe and I also went through a more serious phase of attending political debates and other cultural activities. We had even started to take Russian lessons at evening classes, but this was a limited success. Anyway, I just did not wish to leave anyone with the impression that Joe and I had never done anything useful in Nottingham.

Over the last year, the war had begun to take a very distinct turn in our favour. In 1941 the Germans had treacherously invaded Russia, thus transforming that mighty Opponent into Ally. In December the Japanese attacked Pearl Harbour and so brought the Americans into the war on our side. During 1942 we had recaptured Ethiopia from Italy and in the same year, the British Army under Montgomery decisively defeated the Afrika Korps at El Alamein, the first major Allied victory of the war. Shortly afterwards, British and American troops landed on the coast of French North Africa and advanced to meet up with Montgomery's troops. Simultaneously, the Americans were beginning to turn the tide in bloody combat against the Japanese in the Pacific and an enormous battle was raging in Russia, where the German advance had been decisively halted at Stalingrad and by 1943 a German army corps under Von Paulus was to be totally wiped out. Hitler would not countenance retreat from this hopeless situation, despite the advice of his generals. So millions had to die uselessly and the defeat of the Axis was really getting under way! The Western Allies invaded Sicily and then the mainland and compelled Mussolini's Italy to sign an armistice with the Allies. Mussolini and his pitiful, cowering, bedraggled remnants of an army retreated to the northern half of the country where they continued to hold out with the help of the Germans, but with no great enthusiasm for their cause. For our family, there was one tragic side effect to all this. The political prisoners held on Elba were transferred to prisons in the Alps before the Allies could liberate them and so my brother's incarceration was to endure until nearly the end of the war. Of course, we knew very little about this, except for one or two Red Cross letters received over the years. We had no real idea of what he was going through in all that time.

Chapter 24

FOR ME PERHAPS, John's captive situation had been an added incentive to join the Army and so, having taken leave of our families, Joe and I arrived at Maidstone in Kent to a very rude awakening. Of course, we had heard that the Army was no picnic, but nothing had quite prepared us for our reception. The sergeant who mustered us for onward transit to Invicta Lines (our home from home for the next six weeks), was a raving bully in the best tradition of many Regular Army NCOs. We were marched to our destination, accompanied by the profanities of the aforementioned NCO and there handed over to the sergeant who was to be in charge of our Training Platoon for the next six weeks. He escorted us to our barracks: double tiered rows of bunks along both sides as far as my terrified eyes could see. Everyone dived for what he thought was the most desirable cot and Joe and I did the same. Each cot carried a straw-filled sack called a palliasse, plus two doubtful-looking blankets. Who knows what life was stirring in those palliasses or indeed the blankets.

We were probably the most motley crowd that the Royal West Kent Regiment and maybe the whole Army had ever experienced. It should be noted that we were the first Allied Nationals to be called up to the British Army, so not one of us was British. Secondly, quite a lot could barely understand English, never mind speak it. Our names ranged from relatively simple ones like my own to beauties like Krywiczki and Roizenblatt. Our bewildered Sergeant could neither pronounce our names nor make himself understood. Orders were not so much given as hopefully transmitted. They were then properly debated in English, Polish, German and Yiddish and, with luck, were occasionally acted upon. The sergeant aged visibly in front

of our eyes, and his corporal, until then an innocent young Scot
from Aberdeenshire, was completely at sea. In fact, he might as well
have been. Our new comrades were a miscellaneous lot, made up of
professors, scientists, tailor's apprentices and errand boys, artists,
clerks and just average young guys like myself and Joe, who by the
way was an apprentice draughtsman and could have been exonerated
from military service. Others of our brothers-in-arms had come
straight from London's East End where they hardly ever had to speak
a word of English. There, Yiddish was the lingua franca. Despite
those difficulties in communication, it was made known to us that
we would be most strictly prepared for the rigours of war: ("'Ardships!
you bastards, you don't know what 'ardships are!")

There were pious men and free-thinkers, enlightened liberal intellectuals and people who could not even read or write. Scarcely any two
shared the same belief or opinion. Israel in the making? What particularly got to our NCOs was the fact that two of the men actually insisted
on laying *tefillim* every morning. Picture this: awakened at six a.m. by
the Duty Corporal with ritual shouts of, "Rise and shine, the sun's
scorching your bleedin' eyes out," most of us race out to perform our
ablutions in icy water, in freezing cold huts at least fifty yards away.
But two of our number hold up the war effort because they insist on
laying *tefillim* (phylacteries) and the sergeant wonders mistrustfully
what those men are doing, with wireless aerials wrapped round their
arms and their heads! At least two more men simply will not eat the
traif food. One of them, Krywiczki, effectively goes on hunger strike.
(He was shortly discharged on compassionate grounds, despite the tins
of kosher food that eventually began to arrive.)

Never was there a more slovenly lot and yet, gradually, we were
made to look and behave almost like soldiers. There were exceptions:
characters like Roizenblatt, who used to wet his cot regularly and had
to be awakened with every changing of the guard so he could go for
a pre-emptive pee. He was suitably renamed Roizenbladder. He too

was demobbed in quick time. You could say that he just streamed out
of the Army. A few of us stood out as more promising material, mainly
because we were younger and spoke reasonable English. These included Joe and myself, Private Newman, Private Haas and a few
others. No advantage: we were simply singled out for all the extra jobs
that were going, because at least we understood the orders. Of course,
all of us had to go through a succession of inoculations, injections and
vaccinations which, in my case at least, caused frequent and violent
diarrhoea. Three or four times a night, I would frantically dive off my
top bunk palliasse and charge down the length of the barracks, accompanied by the not-so-gentle complaints of the other inmates. Wearing
just unlaced boots over bare feet and long flannel Army issue underwear under my greatcoat, I would race through the snow to the
lavatories, often arriving, alas, too late. To add insult to injury, my
return to the hut was greeted by a chorus of scatological yells.

Soldier's Service and Pay Book

Thinking back, it seems as if for the whole six weeks of basic training, the camp was covered in a thick layer of snow. We did not so much march as slide on parade, on medical inspection, on training exercises, and to interviews with the Personnel Selection Officer. This individual was usually a well-meaning, bumbling gentleman, who asked you where you thought your future lay in the Army. Some future! Since I was quite aware that I was not much good with my hands and probably not officer material because of my lack of formal education, I pointed out that I was something of a linguist and felt that my best contribution would be in the Intelligence Corps, Sir! The perplexing reply was: "Would you like to be a driver?" Since I could not drive, this appeared a slightly illogical proposal. But then I thought about it and said: "Yes Sir, I would like to be a driver." It seemed a good way to learn. That was the last I heard of this offer and at the end of the six weeks, in keeping with Government policy, I was transferred, together with the majority of my comrades, to the Pioneer Corps. Allied Nationals were only just thought good enough to join a corps consisting mainly of misfits, rejects from most other regiments or from civilian life. There were a few exceptions, like cousin Joe, who was sent to REME because of his technical skills. One of the few round pegs in a round hole. The rest of us went off to Lismore Camp in Buxton, a very pretty spa town nestling in the Derbyshire hills. I won't dwell again on the quality of the troops in the Pioneers. Suffice it to say that by comparison, we new arrivals shone with promise and after a short time were selected to go on an NCO course: specifically Haas, myself and Ernest Newman. Ernest was a natural-born brilliant soldier who stood out head and shoulders above all others. He loved the military life and was, when we later met on leave in London, a dashing, handsome captain in the Parachute Regiment. Anyway, we three passed our NCO course and were duly mustered out as full corporals. Yes, Sir! 13117739, Corporal Kutner N. Sir! The most unforgettable number of my life. They have them in prison too!

I became a drill instructor and marched my squad of Glasgow hooligans and similar dropouts up and down the streets of Buxton. We also did our marching drill while wearing gas masks, an experience not to be commended, particularly when shouting orders at the same time. I lost my voice in the process but still I taught them to march in step, I taught them bayonet drill, I taught them how to handle a Sten sub-machine gun, I taught them rifle drill and in the process tried to learn it myself. I read the men their letters from home and wrote some of the torrid replies to the girlfriends and wives. Off duty I listened to their problems and thanks to my squad, I began to grow up and never had any trouble with any of them, jailbirds and all.

I have not said much about girls. Maidstone had not offered a lot of opportunities in that connection except for a short abortive romance with a pretty nurse whom I had met at a dance. Buxton was different: I got dangerously involved with a beautiful red-head who was also the girlfriend of the regimental Adjutant. If he had caught us, I would surely have found myself courtmartialled and executed by firing squad. I decided that even the beautiful red hair was not worth the risk and that was the end of that!

Then there was Edith Garlick. Contrary to her name, she was fresh and blonde and young and shapely. Her chest was quite remarkable: two exquisite handfuls that in our more intimate moments, she called her swinging bricks. That romance was to last until I shook the dust of Lismore Camp off my boots and headed for a more rarefied atmosphere. But first there was the heady moment when someone up high decided that I might, after all, be Officer Material and I was sent to WOSB (War Office Selection Board). This consisted of three or four days in a requisitioned Stately Home called Locko Park. Here we were tested for our leadership qualities, viz. good table manners, clean fingernails, cultured accent, conversational ability and washing properly behind the ears and perhaps even some military aptitude. We also had to be pretty good at filling in forms and, sort of by the way, had to perform some fairly hair-raising stunts in horrendous weather. In pouring rain we did field exercises which absolutely left me for dead and we performed daring deeds on some kind of flying trapezes in an open-sided gym. The outcome for me was sheer disaster. I could never stay in the air long enough. Then during an interview, I refused the privilege of being considered for an Infantry commission, i.e cannon-fodder, and politely insisted that my four languages qualified me for Intelligence duties. However, the interviewing officer informed me that in Britain, they "could pick people with eight or nine languages off trees"! Oh, the arrant folly of the man! Particularly in view of the much-bruited impending invasion of Europe!

Bloodied, but only slightly bowed, I returned to Lismore Camp and the Pioneers, only to be transferred within days to Kempton Park, London, for immediate attachment to the Intelligence Corps, with the rank of sergeant! K.P. was to be the main reception and interrogation centre for the massive inflow of German Prisoners of War, resulting from D-Day and the assault on the mainland of Europe, which was currently staggering and uplifting the Western World.

Before I come to relate more about Kempton Park, I still cannot resist the petty personal malicious satisfaction of saying to that Major at WOSB: "I told you so!"

I had left Buxton hurriedly but not before ensuring Edith Garlick was kept happily in the family circle by recommending her to my cousin Joe, stationed in nearby Derby. They were lucky that I gave neither of them the German measles which, just a few weeks earlier, had actually caused me to spend a week in a military isolation hospital in Buxton. It could have been worse: at that time we were being deluged with leaflets and film-shows on the dreaded VD, and we all lived in constant fear that it might catch up with us.

Chapter 25

BY THIS TIME, the German air attacks upon Britain had largely receded, thanks to the RAF. People had come out of their shelters and Underground stations and in that sense, life had begun to return to normal. But then, as if to coincide with D-Day, the Germans launched their V1 "Secret Weapon" (*Vergeltungswaffe* = Retribution Weapon). Also soon known as the "Buzz-Bomb" or the "Doodle Bug", it was a small pilotless aircraft that droned and stuttered and puttered its frightening way across the London skies. When the engine cut, it was time to dive for cover! The thunderous silence that ensued was then followed by a great crash, but at least there were a few seconds in which to prepare oneself. I have a cherished memory of our CO diving under the table during a meeting at Kempton Park with his generous bum sticking up in the air. Fortunately for posterior and posterity, the doodle-bug landed some distance away.

For me, Kempton Park was a whole new ball game. The officers and my fellow sergeants were of a very different stamp from the troops I had been with until now. Of necessity, because of the languages, many were also of foreign extraction. But what a great bunch! I formed immediate and long-lasting friendships, in particular with Francis Marsh and Raymond Fenton. Francis was the exceedingly handsome son of a Viennese musical comedy star of the 30s called Hubert Marischka and was himself no mean entertainer. Raymond, also Viennese, was equally handsome and played the guitar. Because of their abilities, they were often asked to entertain at officers' concerts. It made their lives more agreeable and, by association, mine. Raymond Fenton and I are still in touch to this very day, over fifty years later.

The predominant foreign language called for was obviously German, but we also had Russian, Polish and French speakers and several other languages were represented, including my own knowledge of Italian. Our duties consisted of screening the incoming floods of PoWs and selecting the more interesting cases among them for further interrogation. I cannot pretend that our methods were always the gentlest, but at least they never, even remotely, approached the brutality previously displayed under similar conditions by the Germans.

Mainly our captives were Germans and Austrians, but there were also Italians and Russians of many races, including Ukrainian volunteers and Mongolian conscripts. The last were more like slaves than soldiers. A little later there were also quite a few women prisoners, generally much more fanatical and arrogant than the men. One proudly informed me that the words of *Mein Kampf* were engraved on her heart. As for the men, they came to us weary and bedraggled and dispirited. The Kriegsmarine, the paratroopers and the SS were the soldierly exceptions, although the last were careful to try and conceal their SS affiliation. Often they had thrown away their pay books to avoid identification, but unfortunately for them, we quickly discovered that all SS had their blood group tattooed under their left arm and it became standard procedure to order them to strip to the waist for "armpit inspection". Attempts at erasing the offending tattoos were clearly useless and in fact the scars drew our more individual attention to them.

Basically, during those first weeks, we sergeants did the preliminary screening and the officers the more detailed interrogations when deemed necessary. Senior ranks, serious cases of concealed identities, potential war-criminals, and prisoners who might be major sources of information, be they economical, political, scientific or military, were often sent onward to London Cage at Beaconsfield for very well-informed further questioning. For example, one very major objective of our interrogations was to find men who had knowledge of, or had been working at, the Peenemunde rocket research station. The V2 was to become the next "Secret Weapon". Deadly silent, swift and powerful, it landed unheralded and caused widespread death and destruction. It was fortunate for us that the Germans did not have time to perfect this horror weapon till so late in the war. Fortunate too for the Americans, in that they then acquired the services of the German rocket genius Wernher von Braun. He had masterminded Peenemunde and proved a very convenient acquisition in helping them with their Saturn Rocket. How easy when expediency called, to forget that this was the man who had employed and destroyed slave labour on a massive scale and had himself laboured mightily and applied all his genius to the destruction of Britain, America's first ally.

Chapter 26

ON FIRST ARRIVING at Kempton Park we had been simply attached to the Intelligence Division, but shortly afterwards we were properly integrated into the I Corps. Our unit was MI19, Prisoner of War Intelligence. We were all vetted by MI5 and had to sign the Official Secrets Act. Among our officers were some remarkable brains and outstanding personalities. We were under the command of the famous Lt Col. Scotland, formerly a double agent who had even served as a senior staff officer on the German High Command. He later wrote a book on his experiences.

Kempton Park was then a major racecourse, situated at Sunbury on Thames. It had been urgently adapted to our requirements and although we sergeants had to sleep in converted stables, it held many advantages. Its closeness to London made it very possible to get home at weekends when off duty and I was able to see my mother and sister reasonably frequently. Celia had obtained a supervisory position at British Home Stores and was living at Highstone Mansions with Mother.

Occasionally, young American pilots came to call on Celia. For me they were the exciting epitome of glamour and daring, so it seemed doubly shocking to see one of these young men, one night, in a state of high intoxication and not just from drink, give a blow by blow reenactment of one of his missions. He relived his most recent aerial battle, buzzing around our living room with arms extended and was still sweating freely from lingering terror. I was convinced that the following morning he remembered nothing of his performance. It was a shocking insight into what these young men were going through. About a year earlier, Celia's boyfriend of the time, a handsome young giant from the East End, had been killed in action. Not only Celia, but I missed him too; he had been very good to me.

Naturally, only a few of my free weekends were spent with the family. Eve, my girlfriend of the moment, had a sister with a flat in Blackheath and that was a preferred destination. Another flame of the time was Monica. However, once she had been subjected to five minutes of Francis Marsh's concentrated Viennese charm, she was lost to me forever.

Since the extent of our military duties depended mainly on the influx of prisoners, we had some frantically busy spells but also some easy ones. During those lulls we were sometimes able to attend theatre shows in the West End of London which, in the main, were free of charge to soldiers. I affectionately remember Terence Rattigan's "When The Sun Shines", and "The Winslow Boy" starring Eric Portman. I think these were among my first encounters with the charm of the Great British Theatre. I became a victim forever. I also had the pleasure of seeing the fabulous comedian Sid Field at the Prince of Wales Theatre in a show which included Zöe Gail singing "I'm Gonna Get Lit Up when the Lights Go On in London". Bob Monkhouse as a new young stand-up comedian was brilliant and Vic Oliver, Bebe Daniels and Ben Lyon in "Hi Gang" at the London Palladium still hold wonderful memories.

I cannot pretend, can I, that life in the Army was all 'ardships: in fact, I had some very good times. I met lots of girls, mainly at dances. A favourite venue at weekends was the Covent Garden ballroom. Converted from the famous Opera House, it was a very splendid place. There I made the acquaintance of my first American girlfriend: the inimitable Genevieve Holloman, from "good ole sunny Texas". Together with another American couple, we had the heady experience of being thrown out of Quaglino's for making an inebriated spectacle of ourselves. God knows where I found the money, on seventy-five shillings a week! Fortunately, there were also Forces Clubs which were free of charge. At one of these I met Dulcie, a WREN and budding actress. Together we danced to Norrie Paramour and his orchestra. Later I escorted her to her Wrennery and a little later still, I was ejected by an irate Orderly Officer.

On the other hand, we really did great work, most satisfying and interesting. I assisted at very high level interrogations and they were fascinating. Perhaps it was too good to last and rightly so. Out of the blue, some of us were sent on detachment to Devizes in Wiltshire, where we had to process part of the overflowing thousands of prisoners still pouring into the UK. It was quite a good place to be stationed, but London it was decidedly not. It was an incredible experience to see those long straggling field-grey columns of defeated men filing through the streets of Devizes.

Another outstanding memory of Devizes is of the morning we awoke to the drone of many aircraft and on rushing out of our barracks, we saw them: the sky was black with hundreds upon hundreds of glider-towing 'planes heading for Holland and the ill-fated landings at Arnhem. The aerial procession went on and on and was truly an unforgettable sight. Almost exactly fifty years ago today! Very shortly after this we returned to Kempton Park, where normal duties were resumed.

Book 6
With the Army in Europe

Chapter 27

THE ALLIED ARMIES were approaching the German border and we were informed that our services would be required to screen the never-ending flow of prisoners a little more directly behind our advancing troops. With some notable exceptions, those prisoners were now being kept principally in improvised camps on the mainland of Europe. So our detachment, under the command of Lt Morehouse, was ordered to ship out in mid-spring of 1945. We all felt that we were late getting near the action and were champing at the bit. Our initial team of sergeants included McMichael (born Salinger), Morgan (born Meier) Fred Lowry (Commando), Ken Lincoln (Commando) and two later additions were Curly Barry and Bob Reid. My own name was temporarily abbreviated to Kay for security reasons. Under our real names, capture by the enemy might have been distinctly unhealthy.

Just a very few days before our embarkation date, I developed a painful and humiliating case of haemorrhoids. It was not funny! The MO said that I was definitely not fit for active duty and would not be able to embark. This might well have ended my contribution to ending the war that was going to end all wars. So I frantically set out upon a course of self-treatment which in the main consisted of sitting in bowls of near-boiling water and then, when I thought the offending objects had softened a bit, pushing them back into the place from whence they had come. A quick slap of ointment on the relevant spot and voila! a lightning cure and that is the heroic story of how I was still able to join my comrades on our own D-Day and to board the three-ton trucks which from the very start bounced my piles right up into my spine and brain for many agonising miles which made me question my eagerness for action. We finally embarked on a Tank Landing Craft (TLC) to make the grim fearful crossing to Ostend. The danger of air attacks, although blessedly remote, and the much more real bouts of seasickness combined to make me one thoroughly miserable, frightened, pile-encumbered soldier, the butt of everyone's jokes. Ostend, when we landed at least twenty-four hours later, having been held offshore seemingly for ever due to the usual mysterious military reasons and to the stormy weather, was Paradise. From Ostend we proceeded to our first continental POW camp at Vyilvorde, not far from Brussels. Accommodation was in tents pitched in seas of mud just outside the prisoner compound. The screening system here consisted of selecting seemingly trustworthy NCOs from among the captives. They then did the preliminary screening and we did the interrogations. There were thousands upon thousands of these captive men and by now they certainly showed that they knew they were defeated. The work was mostly fairly dull and not really dangerous, although we were not allowed to carry sidearms when working in the compounds. Even armed, we could so easily have been overwhelmed by a mob of prisoners and had our weapons turned against us. On a couple of occasions, inadequately disarmed prisoners did shoot at us as we walked within the camp, thereby giving considerable offence to my highly developed instinct for self-preservation.

Vyilvorde was a dreary little town, but thanks to my French, I soon found myself a welcome guest at the house of a Belgian family and their pretty daughter. (Was it Yvonne?) That friendship lasted for all the time we stayed in Belgium. I was also fortunate to be called upon as interpreter between the camp CO and the mayor on several occasions, and that released me from more boring jobs and gave me some status. Later, our small section was agreeably rehoused in private accommodation. What a war!

VE Day! 8 May 1945. The war in Europe has ended and it seems the whole world is rejoicing. Together with a Belgian fellow sergeant, Albert Lennaerts, who was part owner of a nightclub there, we had made the short trip to Brussels. The streets of the city were packed to suffocation. Everyone wanted to join in the celebrations. Standing room only! There were civilians from all over the country hell-bent on whooping it up. They joined forces with the soldiers, sailors and airmen who were here from every corner of the world: America, South Africa, Britain, India, France, Poland, Canada, Norway, Australia, New Zealand and all other parts of the British Commonwealth and Empire and still more. They all knew that they had a share in this phenomenal victory and they sure meant to celebrate. The cost could be counted later. Meanwhile, we link arms in the streets, and there is dancing where room can be found, on café tables and car roofs and wherever, and we sing. Oh! do we sing! There is a massive wall of sound which pushes all before it, particularly the rousing tones of 'La Madelon' and the cheery din of 'Auprès de ma Blonde'. If you don't know the words, who cares ... Emotions are running high and the Belgian demoiselles are proffering their favours liberally. At last, in Europe, the war is over. Really, truly over!

I arrived back in camp the next morning weary and bedraggled, having bravely fought my way round the back streets of Brussels, with Albert's club as a jumping off place, to realise quickly that my own war had certainly not yet ended. We were ordered to stand by for different duties, in Germany. And so, some days after the end of the war we found ourselves climbing aboard a three-ton truck for our own advance into Germany. As part of my equipment, I still carried those rock-sized haemorrhoids and the three-ton trucks still did nothing to improve them. We also carried with us some very defeated, deflated German generals whom we were to deliver to an advance Intelligence Unit for further questioning. How the mighty had fallen! Here were some of those indomitable generals of the undefeatable German Army, whose reputation we had feared for so long. Now they depended upon us for their very food and most basic needs and even had to ask us nicely to make toilet stops whenever necessary. Mostly, with great glee, we made them pee from the back of the truck whilst in motion. One of the poor guys definitely had waterworks trouble and had to lean out of the vehicle almost constantly, much to our delight. Such petty satisfaction!

One of the generals had belonged to the SS, so it seems proper at this point to put our behaviour and feelings into perspective. At Kempton Park we had speedy access to much very sensitive secret material, which had included horrific photographic evidence of the extermination of the entire population of a small village in western France called Oradour-sur-Glane. It ranks high among the atrocities perpetrated by the Nazis. Oradour had boasted a population of just under one thousand souls. The area SS Commander had "mislaid" one of his senior officers and claimed that the citizens of Oradour had abducted him. Without investigation, he instantly sent his crack troops into the village where they bravely herded the entire population into the church which they then set ablaze. The men were all from the notorious SS regiment "Das Reich". They deployed machine gunners all around the church and waited until the blazing victims tried to panic their way out. As a few succeeded, they mowed them down. Those were the lucky ones. The rest were burned alive. Four people survived this worst of all atrocities. It was only through the Partisans that big glossy photographic evidence reached us so very soon after the event.

Not always did such bestiality go unrewarded: during the eastward evacuation through France of concentration camp inmates from the Channel Islands, a goods train carrying these unfortunate people was intercepted by Canadian troops. When they opened the wagons and saw the dead still standing, packed amongst the living, they simply lined up the German guards and executed the lot. This at least was swift retribution.

Chapter 28

UNDER THE COMMAND of Captain Morehouse our little detachment which now consisted of Sergeants Morgan, McMichael, Reid, Barry and self, had reached Hamburg several weeks after the main body of the Army. Our progress had been slow. We had just zig-zagged from one supply depot to another, from one improvised interrogation room to the next, over roads that had been pretty well mangled up and through towns that were, at least in part, heaps of rubble. The worst experience of all was a brief stop at Belsen Concentration Camp. Although this was a little after the liberation, it was still a nightmare vista. I cannot add to what the world has already seen and heard of this man-made hell, but the picture is imprinted forever on my mind.

Despite having lived through quite a lot of the London Blitz, I was altogether unprepared for my first view of Hamburg: the city had been totally flattened! Standing up in our jeep, it seemed I could see across the whole expanse of the town. The damage we had encountered in the remote wake of the advancing Army was certainly immense in many places, but Hamburg was something else again. Hardly anything was left standing and people were living in the rubble and ruins of the buildings. Tragic latter-day troglodytes. Those were the lucky ones. Thousands of dead still lay under the ruins. On this occasion we spent only a couple of days in Hamburg, but quickly learned that you could have bought anyone, body and soul, in return for a packet of cigarettes. Cigarettes were the staple black market currency, although of course a half pound of butter or a can of coffee ('*Du lieber Tommy, Kaffee*') or a tin of food of any kind served equally effectively. From nowhere, long-hidden cameras and watches and gold coins and all kinds of hoarded treasures suddenly appeared. They were all avidly snapped up, as were the women, who offered themselves freely for the cigarette equivalent of the price of a meal.

These past two weeks, advancing across war-ravaged Germany amid the incredible destruction wrought upon the country and its people, I truly felt that this was a retribution that the Germans had brought upon themselves. For let no one tell you that the Nazis were not a massive majority of the people. Let no one tell you that they did not know of the atrocities that had been going on under their very noses in concentration camps and labour camps. Let no one tell you that they had not heard of the Sonderkommandos who led the systematic destruction of ethnic minorities, particularly in Eastern Europe. Let no one tell you that they did not smile benevolently

At work on Eutin parade ground

upon the atrocious excesses of their monster regime. This was a guilty nation and retribution, if not swift, had been thorough. Belsen avenged, and Auschwitz, and Teresin, and Ravensbrück, and Neuengamme, and all the other organised centres of slaughter. Six million people!

Thousands of German war prisoners, captured during the advance through Germany, had been concentrated in various catchment areas in Schleswig Holstein in northern Germany and it was there we went to continue our screening duties.

First, a pleasant small town called Eutin and then on to Plön, another lovely spot. There we requisitioned a charming little house as our HQ, and settled in to enjoy civilian-style comforts. These comforts included a large carp caught by one of our German minions, which we dumped into our bathtub pending execution. The trouble was, none of us tough soldiers had the bravery to execute sentence, and so far as I know, there may still be an ancient carp called Oskar floating happily in the bathtub of a house in Plön, while the inhabitants have to abstain forever from taking a bath, just as we had to do ...

From Plön, just McMichael, Morgan and I were sent on detachment to a little seaside resort on the Baltic called Pelzerhaken, there to continue the screening procedures. The little village must at one time have been a tiny holiday jewel but it had been transformed into a gigantic encampment: field grey as far as the eye could see, row upon disorderly row of tents, and scattered here and there, a few private villas. On the other side the whole picture was bordered by sand dunes and a wonderful beach, with pre-war bathing huts and basket chairs still scattered around. Quite an idyllic setting, you might say, except that if you cast your glance seaward, past the lovely beach and pretty, romantic bathing huts, you could see a wrecked ship moored some little distance out to sea. What we did not immediately know was that this wreck had been used as a floating concentration camp and had been bombed, in tragic ignorance, by British aircraft. According to the evidence of our own eyes, no one had survived and bodies were still floating ashore daily. By the time they were washed up on our romantic beach, the fish had made a good meal of them and we saw the eyeless sockets and mangled faces of the bloated cadavers. To add to this scene, the British aircraft had been extra efficient because very nearby, a German submarine had been bombed at its mooring. I assume that it had been the original objective of our planes. We thought it would be an adventure to visit this smashed hull. In the event, we went aboard but once and that was enough! The smell was putrid and what we saw inside cured us of any desire to go a second time. All this was quite some weeks after the end of the war.

Thus, from my childhood holiday on the Baltic in the late twenties, I had come full circle to pay another visit, just about sixteen years later. And what changed circumstances! No caring parents now, no frolicking bathers: just some dead, disfigured bodies. And now it was the Army that was in charge of my life, not my parents.

Well, perhaps the Army was not that much in charge. When you send three very young sergeants on a mission like ours, you cannot expect them to keep their collective noses to the grindstone all the time. However, we set up the usual routine: some selected German NCOs did the preliminary screening and then we polished it off, so to speak.

The Army was strictly there to guard the prisoners and to collaborate with us, but we followed our own orders. I was accommodated in a former schoolhouse where I had a large classroom as an improvised bedroom of my own. Among my prisoners, I discovered a tenor who bore the famous name Bruno Walter and I confused him with the real thing. Still, he sang very well and used to come and entertain me and my guests on Sunday mornings. The guests were colleagues, or occasionally some young German lady, including in particular one Gisela, blonde and enthusiastic and ardently cooperative.

In a nearby house overlooking the beach, there lived a rather generously proportioned woman with her husband. She always wore the tightest, shortest shorts possible, which did not attempt to conceal much. Her idea of fun was to entertain the troops, right there in her living room with the great plate-glass windows overlooking the beach, whilst the husband, with his back helpfully turned, played the piano accompaniment. Such sweet music, and so romantic!

On occasion, Gisela and I would sit in those most comfortable deep wicker beach chairs, but this pleasant practice was brought to a very abrupt end by two drunken Army officers who chose to do some impromptu target practice on the beach! Not knowing that we were there, they were happily making the sand spurt all around us, but when they hit the chair itself just above our heads, I felt it was enough. I had not survived the war for this! We started yelling for them to stop.

Eventually they heard us. Since, at that time, fraternisation with German *Fräuleins* was totally *verboten* (a practice anyway only observed in its breach) and I was in a slightly compromising position, my protest had to be somewhat muted. That episode definitely ended any further romantic dalliance on the beach, but did not prevent an interlude with another *Fräulein*, a violinist who was quite eager to do some fiddling. She played altogether the wrong music when she began to tell me how evil were the Jews, and how much she despised them. I asked her, did she know any, and she said, "no, not personally but ..." Her confession of anti-semitism came too late but it tickled my fancy to have had this opportunity of explaining to her the facts of life, in more ways than one.

Soon the Pelzerhaken detachment came to an end and Sergeants McMichael, Morgan and I were ordered to rejoin the rest of the unit and move on to Neumünster. One good thing that had emerged from our stay in Pelzerhaken was that McMichael taught me to drive. This, on a fifteen cwt. Army truck! Not easy! Of course synchromesh was just about unheard of and I had to learn the intricacies of double de-clutching. There was a floor starter button, but more often than not, the truck had to be brought to life with a cranking handle. It sure was a hard way to learn and in the process, I scattered chickens and people with admirable even-handedness all over the roads between Pelzerhaken, Eutin and Plön and on to Neumünster. Here I was to learn in great detail and at first hand about war crimes interrogation. The time spent on these duties was very sadly educational and made a lasting impression upon me. It was another lesson on the subject of man's inhumanity to man.

Chapter 29

NEUMÜNSTER is a medium-sized town in the middle of Schleswig-Holstein, not very far from Hamburg. Here, a gigantic factory-warehouse had been adapted for use as a political internment camp. For the first time, our newly enlarged team was engaged in the interrogation of political prisoners and suspected war criminals. For me, it was an infinitely more satisfying and worthwhile occupation than the prisoner-of-war work. The detainees had been brought in on the basis of their record and rank in the various Nazi organisations, or for their suspected war-crimes. There were high ranking SS officers, leading Party administrators and industrialists, and people whose criminality had been fairly well established or who were to be further investigated. There were also concentration camp doctors and guards and a number of notorious Kapos. Kapos were inmates selected from among the prisoners by the Nazi guards to act as supervisors and spies. They betrayed and ill-treated their fellow inmates in order to feather their own beds. Their treachery often led to the deaths of their poor victims. The Kapos' power was immense. One compound of prisoners consisted entirely of women, again mainly concentration camp guards and other evil fanatical monsters. As ever, the women were the worst, the most arrogant. They were all as one in their lying subterfuge and in passing the buck, but they did not grovel as much as the men. Our task was to satisfy ourselves as to the culpability or otherwise of our prisoners. In those early post-war days, ours was almost a power of life and death over the ones we considered guilty. We could and would often recommend them to be tried for war crimes, which could culminate in the death sentence or long terms of imprisonment.

Again the interrogators were mostly Jewish and of German or Polish origin and I would not deny that we all felt that there was an almost divine retribution in this situation. As concisely as I can, I would like to recount a few of the cases I dealt with. Perhaps you can imagine my own feelings when placed opposite these monsters, in a position of such tremendous power. I am just selecting a few minor examples, because they have not been chronicled as often as some of the major ones.

There was the case of a low-ranking NCO in one of the paramilitary Nazi organisations, the NSKK. His rank certainly did not appear to warrant his arrest. It was unfortunate for him that the records of his home-town Party HQ had fallen into the hands of the advancing British Field Security and included an unsolicited postcard and a letter written by him from Kovno in Lithuania to his local Party boss (*Ortsgruppenführer*). In these he bragged of his participation in the destruction of Kovno's Jewish population. "Dear George, here in Kovno there used to be sixty thousand Jews; now there are only fifteen thousand; still too many of the swine, but don't worry, we'll get rid of them yet. They live in two square metres per Jew and have the nerve to complain about lack of space! Still far too good for them, so each morning we go among them with outstretched arms (rubber truncheons) and finish them off. That'll give 'em room!" There was lots more in that vein, just written to impress. The "rubber truncheon" parenthesis was his.

So we started to question him: No, he had no idea why he had been arrested. He was just an insignificant corporal, just a "little man" (standard justification for their actions) "who would not harm a fly." He had never persecuted Jews, in fact some of his best friends at home were Jews. ("*Die Juden waren meine besten Freunde.*") Many people will recall this standard lie. He strongly disapproved of their persecution and thought firmly that oppressors of Jews should be hung by their necks. Having thus let him inculpate himself, I suddenly shoved his writings at him. He looked, and his face went grey. His body seemed to fold in upon itself like a puppet whose strings have been cut. He appeared to age ten years in that instant. He tried to speak, but could not and had to be supported out by two guards. I never saw him again and do not know what became of him. But you may guess what our recommendation was.

There was the SS man, aged about nineteen, who was accused of shooting, in cold blood, some nine Jews whom he had found hiding in a cellar. He and his comrades simply lined them up against a wall and fired at them with sub-machine guns. Then, just to make sure, he went round the cellar and one by one, he personally and individually fired the *coup de grâce* into their heads. In fact, he had already confessed to eight of those killings. When I pointed out that his file stated that there were nine dead, not eight, he sort of shrugged and said: "It's possible; I may have miscounted, in the heat of the moment." Miscounted! In the heat of the moment! It was one of my few Gentile colleagues, Bill Holmes, who had to be restrained from jumping over the desk to get at him and beat him senseless. These things had been known to happen, but fundamentally we preferred to think that we were better than the brutes who stood before us. Serious manhandling of our prisoners was rare.

Carmen Maria Mori was Kapo of Kapos at Ravensbrück Concentration camp for women. In her thirties, small, dark, not really very attractive, this monster nevertheless possessed a magnetic personality. Ravensbrück Camp was not famous, but Carmen Maria was. Her incredibly brutal history was known even before she came to us.

Interrogating her was an experience. She simply took charge and proceeded to beguile you. It would have been quite easy to fall for her outrageous lies if one had not made a conscious effort to remember that she was a fiend and a sadist, responsible for the brutal ill-treatment and often the deaths of her fellow victims. Inmates who did not instantly do her bidding or who broke any rules, were ruthlessly reported to the Camp authorities when it suited her, with appalling consequences. Unless, of course, they were her protegées. These formed her personal spy network and maintained her in her position of absolute power. Some rendered more personal services, since lesbian activities were very much to the fore. She must have been one of the few prisoners of the Nazis who thoroughly enjoyed her captivity. The tales of skulduggery she related were mind-bending, but of course nothing had ever been her fault. She was said to have accumulated great wealth, but we never discovered where she had "stashed" it. Now, with great fluency, she was informing on all the officials with whom she had previously been so cosy and who had often done her bidding. Very useful, but just the same, she was to be charged with war crimes and we were helping to prepare the case against her. Not easy. She was as slippery as if bathed in oil and when eventually I was transferred away from Neumünster, she was still there, hanging in for dear life ... literally ...

There were obviously hundreds more cases, many of which reached the British press, some making the headlines in a big way. One of these was Irma Grese, commander of the female guards and close colleague of Kramer, the infamous Kommandant of Belsen. She paid us but a short heavily escorted visit before proceeding for more detailed higher echelon interrogation, on her way to the gallows. She was the lady of the human-skin-lampshades, the lady of the jewellery made of gold from the mouths of the dead. There were others just as evil, only less famous. They actually tried to seduce us!

Apart from the occasionally macabre quality of our work, the life we led at Neumünster was positively sybaritic. We had requisitioned a spectacular house, occupied only by our CO and our original team of sergeants. We had our own full-time chef, ex-cruise-ship *Bremen* and our own German household staff. So eager to serve! The chef managed to overcome the problem of food shortages with remarkable ingenuity. Once he parleyed a box of preventatives into a whole calf. On that, we feasted for several days!

I had a splendid room with adjoining bathroom (this was 1945!) and my own Volkswagen. There was no restriction on whom we chose to entertain, since the CO set a fine example in promiscuity. He actually had his German mistress living with him. We had some wild parties and I really did drink too much at that time. Apart from our whisky allocation, our main tipple was Steinhäger schnapps, but anything else we could get hold of was also quite acceptable. Even the household's pet dog, a small white mongrel with black spots, enjoyed a fine taste in alcohol and drank any accessible booze left standing around. Unfortunately, he became alcoholic and began to foam at the mouth. The decision was regretfully taken to put him down, but not one of us five heroes had the guts to shoot him. We delegated this distasteful task to the chef, who did it with one precise shot while we all looked away.

The boys and I soon discovered that being able to understand German was an enormous asset at dances. We would listen to the conversations of the girls and

Neumünster 1946

139

would learn with mathematical certainty what our prospects were for that night ... bingo! bullseye! Another night of easy pickings! I cannot pretend that it was only our uniformed glamour that made us so attractive to the *Fräuleins*: a few cigarettes or a square meal had much greater charms.

It is easy to conclude that we were very irresponsible, but we were young and did have the ball at our feet, so we took advantage. On the other hand, we took our duties and our attitude towards the German prisoners very seriously. We did not allow ourselves to forget what our presence in Germany was all about.

In the autumn of 1945 my mother received, through the Red Cross, the most wonderful yet heartrending letter from my youngest Friedman cousin, ex-Poland. We had thought him dead, but in fact he was the only concentration camp survivor of the family and was now in a DP camp in the American zone of Germany. Subsequently, he also wrote to me. His letter tore me apart. It spoke of his joy at the prospect of finally meeting me, his cousin, and soon the rest of the family. He also said that his health was not good and attempted to describe some of the horrors of the camps.

My mother had urgently requested permission of the American Occupying Force in Germany to visit him, and this was granted. But this longed-for family reunion was not to be. Whilst she was feverishly preparing for her journey to Germany, Mother received official notification from the Americans that my cousin had succumbed to TB contracted in the camps. Of the tragedies and heartbreaks suffered because of Nazi violence, this single, terrible event hit home most of all. Now it only remained for us to hope for better news of John.

Chapter 30

I HAVE NOT MENTIONED my brother for some time, because since his removal to the fortress of Saluzzo in the Italian Alps, there had been no news of any kind, despite continued efforts by the International Red Cross. Things had been made more difficult as he had no address for us in the UK. But then, late in 1945, at last, a letter! He was well and living in Saluzzo, the very town where he had been incarcerated. It was like having him back from the dead. The excitement! It was just wonderful! I immediately applied for compassionate leave to visit him. This was eventually granted and in December my adventurous journey began. I was longing to see John and hear the story of his imprisonment and adventures and I was not to be disappointed.

But first, to get to Saluzzo! Lugging my kitbag and two squeaky-clean blankets, I climbed aboard a broken-down troop train in Hamburg, heading for Holland and Belgium. After nearly two days of interminable stops, via Copenhagen and goodness knows where else, we finally reached Brussels where I had to change trains. From bad to infinitely worse! Nearly another three days of travel through Belgium, France and Switzerland into Italy. This time there was no heating, not that it would have done much good; most of the compartment windows were smashed anyway. There was little water and even less food. While the train kept stopping, we just sat there, huddled in our blankets and our misery. Hygienic facilities were almost totally unheard of.

One freezing dawn we arrived at yet another stop, high up in the Alps somewhere between France and Switzerland. On what must have been the coldest, most miserable morning of my entire life, we were ordered to alight from the train and then shepherded to the lavatory facilities. These consisted of twin footrests, each pair straddling a primitive hole in the ground, the contents of which were frozen in all their obscenity. The whole place was covered by a rusty corrugated tin roof, which surely was going to take off any minute as the numbing Arctic wind just kept on shrieking through it. For washing purposes, we were kindly offered large water barrels standing beside the so-called ablution hut, but first it was hand-numbingly necessary to break through thick layers of ice in the barrels. Well, when you are young, anything is sustainable, but sometimes only just. We grumbled our way back onto the train and then, with frozen faces scraped raw by our razors and hands and noses turned respectively blue and red by the icy water, our weary bodies were finally carried onward through peaceful, undamaged, unbelievably lovely neutral Switzerland. Still being in uniform, we were not allowed to leave the train until we reached Italy.

At last, Milan! Then the excited search for the train to Saluzzo via Cuneo. Bless and double bless my knowledge of Italian! It just about propelled me to Cuneo, the last way-station boasting a small British garrison. I had been instructed to report there: of course, on arrival, no one had ever heard of me. Nevertheless I was issued with loads of supplies and eventually found myself on the local train to Saluzzo, weighed down by all the scarce, precious tins I was carrying, evidently the first British uniform to be seen in the area for a very long time.

Conquering hero, I steamed into Saluzzo and there on the platform, attended on either side by a lovely signorina, stood my brother John! The train squealed to a halt right there beside him. Laboriously lugging all my equipment, I clambered down. After seven years, a long war and a terrible journey for me, it was unbelievable to hear my big brother's voice. And these were his immortal words: "God, how grown up you are! Now we can go after the women together! The one on my left is for you." Talk about anticlimax!

And so, we made our way through narrow, hilly streets where I was amazed and flattered to see both our names splashed on walls all over the place: "Viva Jean," "Viva Bob." You can imagine my curiosity: what had made me such a hero? Or him? When we finally reached his place, I settled down eager to hear it all, but I only got a bit at a time; somewhat like Boccaccio's *Decameron* or more likely, *The Thousand and One Nights*. We kept being interrupted by the girls and by a stream of visitors. They had heard of my arrival and turned me into an instant celebrity. As the only British soldier around, I became a superstar, promptly promoted to Capitano. Everyone wanted to pat me on the back. I was the liberator! But that was not the real cause of my undeserved popularity. The main reason was to emerge from my brother's tale.

Chapter 31

JOHN'S TALE: when he was arrested in Milan back in 1938, he was actually on his way home and had no idea of the trouble he was in. His arrest in the street, right outside our apartment block, was like a bombshell. His world collapsed, but still he did not realise that he would be spending the next several months in gaol awaiting trial. He did eventually become aware that Mother was working frantically on his behalf just trying to secure the services of a lawyer to defend him, but as I mentioned earlier, without money or connections liberal defenders were an endangered species. With her usual heroic persistence, she found a man brave enough to take such a case, and for little or no reward. John was becoming frighteningly aware that there was no hope of getting off lightly. Nonetheless, when it came, the thirty year sentence savagely inflicted upon him was beyond his worst nightmare. The end of his world. Unimaginable ... thirty years!

No remission for good conduct! Fifty years old when he would finally be released ... abandon hope, all you who enter ... the verdict had followed the Judge's remark that as a foreign Jew he was lucky not to be sentenced to death!

They sent him to the island of Elba, to be kept there, imprisoned and often chained and in solitary to begin with. No visits from outside, except for the one from my mother. Not that anyone else was likely to come calling. Later, he shared a cell. His cell-mates were the only human contact. Like him, they were "politicos", mostly sentenced for left-wing anti-Government activities. They gradually converted him to their political persuasion. In his receptive frame of mind, that must have been easy. They passed the crawling time with political and philosophical discussions and even taught each other languages, so that to his fluent knowledge of German, French and Italian, John added excellent English and some Yugoslav and Spanish. Of his time in Elba, he would not tell me much more, except that conditions were awful, not helped by the war with its cruel shortages. Then came 1943 and Mussolini's débâcle. John and his cell-mates were removed to Saluzzo, where things looked just as hopeless. From an island fortress to a mountain stronghold, from a rock to a bloody hard place.

But then, in 1944, came the first ray of hope, the first chink of light. The Italian Partisans were beginning to be very active. Largely ardent Communists, they were set to undermine the already weak Fascist rule. They were swarming all over the mountains around Saluzzo and guerilla fashion, attacking the Germans and the loyalist Fascist troops wherever they could find them. Their nuisance value was growing all the time and to boost this, they were always on the lookout for volunteers. When John secretly received a message that he was to report sick to the prison hospital, he had a good idea what this meant. Freedom was close! A doctor, sympathetic to the partisan cause, informed him to his astonishment that he had just developed serious appendix trouble and that an urgent operation was vital. This was news to John. Just like that, a life-threatening situation! The sham surgery was quickly performed and before the scar even had any chance of healing, the partisans spirited him out of hospital and hey presto: meet my brother the guerilla!

What follows was told to me not by him but by one of his former comrades, not that modesty was John's greatest virtue. Under his *nom-de-guerre* of Jean, he had teamed up with another partisan named Bob and together they had pulled off some incredible exploits. They had calmly bicycled into enemy positions and shot up everything and everyone in sight. Then they had removed such weaponry as they could carry and disappeared into the night. The daring of their actions is perhaps best illustrated by the cruelty and torture that the two sides inflicted upon each other with remarkable even-handedness if and when they took prisoners. Their preferred method was to shoot on sight. Otherwise, one of the favourite German treatments was to make the prisoner strip naked and seat him upon a red-hot stove until he talked. Eventually they were executed anyway, since the Germans did not recognise guerillas as regular troops, and the guerillas naturally played tit-for-tat.

Meanwhile, Bob and Jean kept up their activities for several months, in and out, in and out until, together, they were captured. Both were due to be executed; both were saved, miraculously, by the ending of the war. By now, the Nazis and the Fascists had neither the appetite nor the courage for tortures and executions. They had enough trouble guarding themselves against similar acts of vengeance by the partisans. So, truly free for the first time, Jean and Bob found themselves celebrated heroes of the valleys. Their fame had spread before them. Now I knew why "my" name had been daubed all over the place, alongside John's. No hero I; but to these people of the mountains, John really was. He had been imprisoned: he had almost fallen for the Cause: he had fought the great fight.

Chapter 32

ELSEWHERE, mighty things were happening. Hitler, threatened by the advance of the Russians into Berlin, had committed suicide in the Führerbunker with his wife Eva Braun, thus encountering the miserable end he so richly deserved. The city of Berlin, smashed by Allied bombs and Russian artillery, created the correct setting for Hitler's personal damnation. The world had hoped for this kind of conclusion, but no one had really ever dared believe that the Nazi shout would end in such a whimper. Others of his gang died with Hitler in the bunker, including the vile liar Göbbels and his vast family. Many of the others were arrested and subsequently charged with war crimes at the Nürnberg trials, where one in particular, fat Hermann Goering, escaped justice by swallowing cyanide. His famous slogan during the war had been: *"Kanonen anstatt Butter"* (Cannons instead of butter) but for Hermann there were never any shortages. Earlier I had been lucky enough to be on the fringes of some of his interrogations. It was an immensely interesting experience. Highly educational! Others who committed suicide were Hitler's deputy Martin Bormann (although some still think he had escaped and disappeared for good) as well as the arch evildoer Heinrich Himmler, chief of the dreaded Gestapo. Amongst the others to stand trial were the villainous Ribbentrop, former ambassador to Britain, and Funk, and Streicher, anti-semitic propagandist supreme. Many more were able to make their escape, mainly to South America where there were a host of Nazi sympathisers. This was often achieved with the help of the "Vatican pipeline" which was instrumental in spiriting people like Joseph Mengele, the Angel of Death of Auschwitz, Adolf Eichmann and other monsters like them to freedom. The Vatican's complicity in these activities was amply demonstrated. Even clearer was the active antisemitism of the Papal State. Never did it lift a finger or raise its voice in defence of Jewry. To this day this is the subject of much discussion and research. Plays have been performed and books written on the topic. It is good that the scandalous proceedings of Pope Pius XII and the devious Catholic hierarchy of that time should be thus remembered.

Mussolini's collapse naturally coincided with that of his boss. Not for him the possible exaltation of what Hitler may have seen as his own *Heldentot.* In shabby looking civilian clothes, wearing a slouch hat to help prevent recognition, he had tried to steal away into the night, together with his mistress Clara Petacci. They were both caught by the Partisans and Il Duce's ignominious life was ended in ignominious fashion, hanging by his ankles from a lamp-post in Milan's Piazzale Argentina. His mistress was made to keep him company and so they swung, side by side, to the delight of the suddenly virulent Anti-Fascists who stopped to jeer where they had for so long cheered.

Writing about the horrific extinction of Hitler and Mussolini, brings to mind the very relevant astonishing story of an eminent Italian nuclear physicist, Enrico Fermi. In 1928 he had married a Signorina Laura Capon who happened to be Jewish. In the religiously liberal Italy of those days, no one thought anything of it although it was a most unlikely alliance, as there were one thousand times more Catholics than Jews living in Italy. However, by late 1938 when he was due to travel to Stockholm with his whole family to receive the award of the Nobel prize for his outstanding work in nuclear physics, things had changed considerably. He was painfully aware that there was nothing left for him in an Italy where his children and his wife would now be the probable victims of religious persecution. As you can see, it did not just happen to lesser mortals like myself. Laura Capon's father, the former chief of Italian naval intelligence, had been demoted and disgraced and later died an old man at Auschwitz.

Signor Fermi wisely decided not to return to Italy at all from Stockholm, but to proceed direct to the United States. Within four years of arriving there, Fermi had designed the first atomic reactor. It became "critical" in December 1942 and proved to the Americans, beyond reasonable doubt, that atomic bombs were a realistic proposition and in fact, the Americans immediately put their atom bomb programme into full swing. Two and a half years later, two atomic bombs were dropped on Hiroshima and Nagasaki, thus ending the war in Japan. The irony is that, had Mussolini not introduced his antisemitic laws, Fermi would have had no reason to leave Italy. He would almost certainly have produced the atomic bomb for the Axis at Joachimstal in the Sudetenland instead of in Chicago. 19 July 1928, the day of Fermi's marriage, must therefore be a most significant one, as it undoubtedly helped to change the history of the world.

Chapter 33

IN THE CHARGED post-war atmosphere in Italy, John found himself back in civilian life. Pampered and courted by the Communists, presumably because of his recent history, he had been made editor of the local weekly paper in Saluzzo and had also been called upon to make fiery speeches on behalf of the "Party". Indeed, he lived a very active political life in those months after the war. However, nothing altered the fact that he was chronically short of money, so he also appointed himself as his own sports writer. Presumably these glittering literary activities kept him going, supplemented, albeit briefly, by my Army goodies which we flogged on the black market. Socially, he did appear to have a great life and I shared in it during my short stay. On the other hand, because of his political leanings and the Italian temperament, he was often engaged in violent arguments with the opposition. This even carried over into his newspaper writings. After a particularly heated discussion with an opponent who happened to be a ladies' hairdresser he styled him in his paper as, the "*barbiere donnaiuolo*". This unwarranted description of "womanising barber" caused great affront to his adversary and led to pushing and pulling and scrapping in a restaurant and suddenly I thought how adult I was by comparison with my big brother. So I watched, but carefully kept out of it and just continued to enjoy myself in every possible way during my remaining time in Saluzzo.

Too soon, I had to leave John and return to the Army. My planned leave however included one full day of freedom in Milano. Wonderful! Nostalgia with a capital N! I revisited school friends from so many years ago and was mainly rewarded with warm welcomes. The girls were flattering and the guys very friendly. One of the mums even invited me to dinner and to spend the night at their home. I suppose it was strange: the former classmate and friend, now a soldier in an alien army, with a whole war in between.

An important disappointment was my visit to Professor Rossi. When I rang his bell, the door just opened to a few suspicious inches. All I was allowed to see was half his face. Curtly he said, "Yes, I remember you. You were always a good boy." And he closed the door. In a country full of post-Mussolini and post-war blood-lettings and vendettas, he may well have had greater worries than me to contend with. He looked nervous. Perhaps he was startled by my uniform. When I was drummed out of school, it was he who had encouraged me to become a writer. I fear he would have been horrified to read this, my belated inadequate first response.

I spent that night with the Massone family and next morning I was able to pay a visit to my father's grave at the Musocco cemetery. I was elated to find that a handsome tombstone had been erected in his memory. Thank you, Uncle Jack. Then swiftly I embarked on a considerably easier return journey to Neumünster and took up my duties where I had left off.

Our interrogation work was continuing intensely as before, with much the same senior team under the command of Major Morehouse. It is notable that he had engineered his promotion from Lieutenant to Captain and then to Major since Kempton Park, whilst we, his hard working staff, had all remained sergeants and he happily kept us firmly rooted there while we did all the work. Generally, it went quite well, although not without some criticism, mainly from the bleeding-heart British press. Wringing their lily-white hands in their anxiety for British justice, they bleated loudly about their concern for the well-being of our poor Nazi war criminal internees. They felt that some of the questioning was not done sufficiently tenderly and according to Hoyle and that the calories *per diem* allocated to the prisoners were not adequate. Oh, shades of Oranienburg,

Huchenwald, Belsen, Auschwitz, Dachau! It is worth remembering that the people at home were still undergoing very stringent food rationing, hardly any better than the prisoners. What a pity we did not have the right of reply!

As the year 1946 went by, it became very clear that some of the bigger fish in the former Nazi Party were beginning to receive kid-glove treatment at the sub-rosa behest of our own authorities. De-Nazification was becoming a hollow laugh. The Allied Powers needed the major Nazi industrialists, scientists and leading personalities (mostly Nazis) to rebuild German industry and at the same time, form a bulwark against the Russians whose might was very much feared by the West in general and the Germans in particular.

The off-duty life, however, continued to be amazing and I managed to get into many scrapes. Not always trivial, I'm proud to say. On the other hand, like a good boy I wrote frequently to my mum and wish now that I had kept her replies, since they were an excellent commentary on the times.

Our leisure activities were mainly, as ever, the pursuit of the ladies. Well, not really so much a pursuit. We also played a lot of poker, a game I enjoy to this day, and our stakes were cigarettes, still the principal currency of the moment. My salary as a sergeant was, and at its peak remained, the princely sum of 75 shillings per week and that did not build a great reserve fund for me when I finally got home on leave. But home I went, having first survived the brutal sea-sickness of a North Sea crossing from Cuxhaven to Hull.

It was during this leave that Topsy came into my life. On a lonely evening, I had gone to the Astoria Ballroom in Charing Cross Road in the hope of unearthing some talent. I was in luck! She was seated at a table behind some artificial shrubbery on the Balcony floor. I mustered the celebrated courage that had helped me fight my way round the backstreets of Brussels and made some highly witty and original remark about hiding her light behind a bushel. Surely such drollery could not fail to impress and indeed Topsy was clearly stunned and overwhelmed by it, so much so that when I asked her to dance, she quite lost her power of speech and just shook her head in the negative. A little later I felt I should give her another opportunity, so I tried again. This time she had recovered sufficiently to say: 'Thanks, but no thanks.' If the girl simply did not know what was good for her, there was nothing more I could do.

I wandered away and that might have been the end of that, but we ran into each other a couple of dances later. This time, with sweaty, nervous hands clutched behind my back, I simply asked if she would dance and she said yes! A quick surreptitious wipe of the hands down the side-seams of my trousers and off we went. And off indeed we went! The rest of that leave was spent closely together and in due time she actually joined me in Germany, having enlisted in the newly formed CCG (Control Commission for Germany). But more, much more of that, in due course.

Chapter 34

MUCH TOO SWIFTLY my home leave came to an end. Topsy and I bade each other a reluctant, tearful farewell and I reported to the troopship that was to return me to Cuxhaven. As I was going up the gangplank, very properly minding my own business, I was nabbed by a CSM who assigned to me the duty of Mess Deck Sergeant. What a choice! The ship set out and I reported to the mess-deck at just about the time when the going got rough. The men promptly started to spill their food or throw up all over the place. I took one look and not to be outdone, proceeded to throw up right where I stood. The entire rest of the crossing was spent in the ship's sick bay. No thought of romance now, my only preoccupation being to keep death at arm's length, which at the time I thought improbable. But I must have succeeded because, to my surprise and in no time at all, I was back at work in Neumünster. The Army did not have to dispense with my services after all.

Of course, much had happened outside my own little sphere since our northward travels through Germany in the early summer of 1945. Japan had surrendered in September of that year as the result of the two atomic bombs dropped on the hitherto barely known Japanese towns called Hiroshima and Nagasaki. The civilian populations of these doomed cities were all but burned to a crisp. This operation was loudly acclaimed by all, who felt the Japanese had brought it upon themselves and they had only got what they amply deserved and that at least it had ended the war more quickly. Thus we all reasoned then. But as time passes, we ask ourselves if slaughter on such a scale for whatever purpose can ever be justified. On the one hand there had already been the Allied bombings of Dresden and

Hamburg and Berlin. On the other, the Germans had just about invented it all with the Blitz on London and Coventry and many other cities. And then again, there was the indescribable brutality of the Japanese and their barbaric treatment of prisoners. Many, many thousands of Allied personnel died of beatings, disease and starvation, including uncounted women and children. Now, just about fifty years afterwards, we think we have all the answers. Now we say none of the frightfulness of the atom bombs and all the other bombings should have been allowed to happen. But then we recall the bestiality of the Nazis and the horror of their concentration camps. Should that have been allowed to go unpunished? Meantime, nothing has been learned and the butchery goes on. Now we have the troubles in Yugoslavia, in Rwanda, in parts of the new Russia, in Angola and wherever religious, racist or tribal fanatics can hold sway.

The immediate sequel to the Concentration Camps were the Displaced Persons (DP) Camps. Established by the Allies to house the surviving victims of the Holocaust, they were nevertheless not exactly luxury hotels and created quite fierce resentment among the DPs, who felt that they had been confined long enough and rightly showed their frustration. We frequently visited one such tented camp outside Neumünster and found there a sense of mounting resentment even against their very Liberators. The people wanted to be free, to get away, to Palestine, Britain, America or wherever else they were allowed in and that was very difficult. Still nobody wanted them. And so history repeated itself. Where to go, where to go? ...

Some of the DPs had begun to try and make a life for themselves locally and thus at a Sergeants' Dance, I came to meet a very beautiful Lithuanian girl who had already been lucky enough to set up her own home in Neumünster. She was tall and very shapely. Every step she took was like a celebration of her freedom. Seeing her joyful, long-striding walk was like watching spring. It was because of her that I nearly became involved in a very real gun-fight, Another sergeant claimed to have prior rights over the lady and threatened me with a revolver when he found us alone together in her rooms. That was absolutely no kind of ending for this Jewish boy! Fortunately, this charade led to an instant stand-off and my rival retired with welcome haste. I was certainly more scared at that instant than at any time during the actual war!

The young lady and I became very close for a little while and Topsy faded swiftly from my mind. I am definitely not making excuses for myself. I was young and very selfish, and if I were to apologise for my lively life-style during that period, I would have to do so at least a dozen more times for a dozen equally delicious reasons. There were the German twins, not beautiful but adventurous and the voluptuous redhead called Annemie. There was the occasional reappearance of Gisela and also a slightly older woman called Ilse, whose husband had shared the fate of so many other Germans and disappeared in Russia. Ilse probably thought it jolly sporting of him, since she was also my CO's girl-friend and shared her favours very generously between us, although he was kept happily unaware of our mutual partnership. Where ignorance is bliss ... Somehow it seemed right to avail myself of all those glistening opportunities; the expression "Male Chauvinism" had not yet been coined.

Once again, I must stress that we played hard but we also did a great deal of work. It was interesting and for those with my background very rewarding. We continued with the questioning of people whose names are recorded in history for their infamy and others who only made their minor personal contributions to the evil that had just been brought to an end.

Another home leave came along and back to London I went. I saw Mother and Celia at Highstone Mansions and took up with Topsy where we had left off. She informed me joyfully that she had been accepted for the Control Commission for Germany as an IO3,

Intelligence Officer Grade III, and would be arriving shortly at Bad Oeynhausen, HQ of the British Army of Occupation. I experienced mixed emotions, since I had just received orders to rejoin my unit, not at Neumünster but at our new base at Sennelager II, near Bielefeld, which happened to be perhaps just a bit too close to Topsy for comfort.

At Sennelager our house was not as luxurious as the last, but we had even more German staff to provide us with the comforts to which we had become so agreeably accustomed. Our CO no longer shared our quarters. He was mostly to be seen driving around in his magnificent requisitioned drop-head Mercedes, with his large Alsatian in the back-seat and a suitable blonde in the front. Or was it the other way round? We had brought our chef with us and he continued his culinary miracles. The village of Sennelager was small, and its activities revolved mainly around our slightly enlarged unit and that of a Field Security Section stationed there, plus the back-up troops. The village boasted a manual petrol pump (out of use), an inn, a little village hall and maybe a hundred houses. We had a daily journey of a few kilometres to the internment camp, where our duties were mainly unchanged, although of course our "clients" were all new to us, This covered the period late 1946 to my demob in July 1947.

The Grand Duke of Mecklenburg, a remote cousin of the King, was one of our "guests". He actually received occasional gift packages of food from the British Royal Household, but I am ashamed to say that the Camp Staff managed to "lose" most of the contents. There were complaints and enquiries but they met only with blank stares. I had to question the Duke often, because there was great outside pressure for his release. I found him a quiet man, whose arrest was mainly due to his automatic high honorary rank in the SS, which Hitler had thrust upon many of the Nobility for the sake of appearances. It is a fact that, in common with most of the German upper crust, he had scant time for the "little Austrian". Indeed, it was his "class" that tried to blow up Hitler in July 1944. Another representative of the nobility among my clients was Count von Reventlow, who had also suffered from the automatic rank of SS Standartenführer. He was a cousin of Lance Reventlow, one of Barbara Hutton's succession of husbands. I could truly find no case to bring against him and used him as a personal assistant, pending his eventual release. This was entirely a routine matter, but he seemed to feel indebted to me and wrote me a fulsome letter of thanks and later sent me several invitations to his castle in Schleswig Holstein. Eventually I accepted and in the course of a holiday jaunt with Topsy, I was able to visit for a few hours.

The Reventlow home was the original fairytale castle, complete with turrets, moat and drawbridge in perfect working order. The baronial hall itself was festooned with ancient battle-flags and tapestries and the interior was quite shabby and neglected. You felt you could blow it all away with a powerful puff. Since my selection of friends included only a few who owned medieval castles, the experience was overwhelming and on the way out I kept wanting to turn back and ask Rapunzel to let down her long hair. My host must have relished the occasion, because for years afterwards, he wrote to me precisely on the anniversary of that visit and on the anniversary of his release from internment.

Whilst I was completing my last year in the Forces, indulging in far too much wildness and occasionally even work, my brother was getting into all sorts of trouble of his own, back in Italy. His stint as a big-shot in the Communist Party was coming to a close. Being fired at for your point of view while making political party speeches in Sicily was no job for this tired ex-hero and it was thought prudent to remove John to healthier climes. It also seemed that he was no longer *persona grata* with the Italian Government and so an elaborate procedure was set in motion by the Communist Party to supply him with a false identity. It all took a long time, and for a while he seemed to disappear. When he eventually re-emerged, he was no

The Under-Secretary of State for
War presents his compliments and
by Command of the Army Council
has the honour to transmit the
enclosed Awards granted for
service during the war of
1939-45.

CAMPAIGN STAR

No....14147372........ Rank..Sgt........... Name.........XUTTER......
of this unit is entitled to........France and Germany Star......
so far as I can ascertain without reference to GHQ 2nd Echelon by virtue of the
B.L.A., 1 May – 8 May 45.
following service:-

Signed...................
O., Det.C.S.D.I.C. (UK)att. 8 Corps

B.L.A.   19 July
Date...........................1945

longer Horst/Jean/John/Kutner, but "G.T.", a man who had died not very long ago in action and whose documents showed him to be just a few months older than John. He would have had to be someone who had no family and was generally anonymous.

Not so very long after I was demobbed, John appeared in Britain under his new name and spent more than a year in this country, staying partly with Celia, partly with Mother or me. He had definitely left his old life behind and incidentally renounced his Jewishness totally and permanently. Now he committed himself to studying electrical engineering at the London Polytechnic. After one year during which he did very well, he scraped together enough money to help him work his passage to Brazil. First though, he was joined in London by Lillina, one of the girls who had come to meet me in Saluzzo, and eventually they married. They had a son, but divorced soon after. My unknown nephew must now be at least in his middle forties. To the best of my knowledge, both he and his mother went back to live in Italy. I have since discovered that Lillina died of cancer.

In Brazil John married for the second time. She was a beautiful woman I knew only from photographs and they had a girl and a boy, Claudia and Fabio. She died without really seeing her children grow up and much later he married for a third time, a dusky beauty called Ararita. At the age of fifty-six, he had a gorgeous blonde daughter and quite seriously stated that he thought he would perhaps not have any more family! Enough was enough ...

Barbara and I met him after a very long separation, on a visit to Rio. For Barbara it was the first time. He now lived in modest retirement in a town not far from Sao Paulo, surrounded by wife and children, and at least three grandchildren. We corresponded only sporadically, but since Mother died in her nineties about four years ago and Celia of a brain tumour about eighteen months ago, we two and my son Tony are the only Kutner survivors, under whatever name.

Chapter 35

To RETURN TO MY MILITARY SERVICE: I have to admit this was getting less and less motivating all the time. There were two main reasons. The first was that all my old colleagues were being demobbed one by one and replaced by low-grade Control Commission officials who could not, even with a major effort, distinguish a German Panzer from a perambulator or a war criminal from a fairy godmother. At best they spoke schoolboy German and understood nothing of the background history. And anyway, how could they possibly replace my buddies? – McMichael the schoolteacher, who was the only one to exercise a restraining influence on me; Morgan, the intense bespectacled character who foresaw the end of the world at every turn and who eventually emigrated to Australia; Curly Barry, ex-Hamburg and East End of London, who spoke both languages with the very strong flavour of Aldgate and Reperbahn and whose renderings of songs from both cities were a riot. Barry it was who discovered that his girl friend of the moment was pregnant and felt assured that if she drank enough gin and took boiling hot baths and jumped down long flights of stairs, she would without doubt miscarry, to their mutual relief. So we all stood at the bottom of this long flight of stairs to break her inebriated falls and, when her period did arrive just a little late, he was convinced that they had beaten the system. All this, incidentally, in our official billet. I must not forget Bob Reid, who gave unstinting support to all my escapades and who remained my friend long after the Army. And of course we were all poker-playing companions. To see them gradually replaced by people from civilian life was strongly resented.

The second and more serious reason for my growing lack of interest was that our interrogations were becoming more and more futile. So-called Review Boards had been formed consisting mainly of ex-Indian Army officers who were supposed to pass judgment on our recommendations. Their purpose, plainly, was to release as many Nazis as possible in order to strengthen the Allied stance against Russia and take major positions in the rebuilding of the German economy. We felt let down and betrayed and none of this was helped by the fact that those elderly relics of the first war thought that some of the prisoners were really jolly good chaps; if they spoke English, which many of the Nazis did, then evidently they could not be all bad. It goes without saying that very few of the Review Officers had even a microscopic knowledge of German or any kind of understanding of recent German history. How our clients must have laughed on their way out of internment, with practically clear sheets or perhaps a rap on the knuckles or at worst a recommendation to go through the denazification progress. After all, they had only tried *en masse* to get rid of the Jews and other such low elements.

It is interesting to note that now, some fifty years after, many of the Nazis or their heirs who benefited from this gentle treatment are in leading positions in German industry and finance. And so much of this is based, softly-softly, on the old evil fraternity of Nazism.

Book 7
Home and Away

Chapter 36

O N LEAVING THE ARMY I received what was laughingly described as a gratuity. This was the sum a grateful government bestowed upon its fighting men in recognition of, in my case, four years of lost youth. Well, perhaps not exactly lost youth, as I mostly enjoyed a very good time in the Forces and took very dedicated care not to expose myself to serious danger. In common with all the others, I did however lose that precious time to prepare for my future. Be that as it may, the princely amount of the gratuity was two hundred and seventy-some pounds. When added to the money I already had, this still made a total of two hundred and seventy-some pounds.

Richly attired in my herringbone demob suit of wood and wool mixture, I took my first steps to conquer the commercial world. The commercial world did not seem to notice and so I joined my sister Celia in a venture known as Cut Make and Trim (CMT), in which it seemed she had acquired some skills. Imaginatively, we named this enterprise C&B Fashions and she added her accumulated capital to mine, so that together we now had the sum of two hundred and seventy-some pounds. The point of the exercise was to convert dress fabric supplied by clothing manufacturers into finished ladies' garments, for which service we received an inadequate fee. That is, when we were able to obtain any work at all. Clothing coupons were still in force with the consequent limitation upon the number of garments that could be produced, at least legally. Our venture soared like a kite. Sadly, in keeping with the old axiom, what goes up must come down and indeed we did, rapidly.

My friends thought that this work was not in keeping with my superlative talent and appearance and I modestly agreed with them.

They felt I should do something much more ambitious, but then advice was the only thing that came free. I did however develop another interest: my sister Celia had struck up a great friendship with another Celia, the wife of famed night-club owner, entertainer and comedian Al Burnett. So, through the good offices of Celia's C&B, I found myself employed as under-manager of the renowned Stork Club in the West End of London. Al felt I was the only man he would trust with the takings, perhaps an indication of the fragile reliability of his staff. All this opened up a whole new world to me. I still did my daytime stint at C&B Fashions in Camden Town while it lasted and then from 10 p.m. to 6 a.m. I spent with the people who made up this new underground twilight world: Pip, the Maître d'; the other waiters; the cloakroom girls, one of whom, absolutely gorgeous, applied herself to making my life in the nether regions of Conduit St, W1, even more appealing; the entertainers, the musicians, the chorus, the strippers, more romantically described as exotic dancers, and all those performers of stylised, witty and slightly decadent songs at the piano, *à la* Noel Coward. And to top them all of course, the unique, inimitable Al. I just loved my life here behind the scenes of the nightclub entertainment world. Move over, Toulouse Lautrec!

So, Ladies and Gentlemen, your Host, Mr Al Burnett!

"Did I tell you, ladies and gentlemen, how I met my wife? There she was, standing outside a pawnbroker's shop picking her teeth and I went inside and helped her pick the teeth she wanted. She was gloriously beautiful, She was wearing a brown dress with a white lace collar: she looked like a glass of beer with legs."

Music: "But you should get her, in a sweater, even two little fried eggs look better ..." Music ends: more patter ...

All clever daring stuff ... I'm sure you've got the idea! Visitors to the club included the great Danny Kaye, comedienne Martha Raye, who had played opposite Charlie Chaplin in a major film, Lena

Horne and several other beautiful leading ladies. Do I need to repeat how much I loved it all? When they came round to the club after their shows, they either just dined there or did a bit of entertaining. They were all famous Hollywood stars who, with their fresh wit and talent and the latest in entertainment from New York, were taking the London theatres by storm.

We had regular upmarket amateur spots, hugely looked forward to by the performers: Mr Five-by-Five Len Mittelle, bookmaker, whose enormous girth occupied just about the entire stage and who insisted on singing "All of me, why not take all of me"; the titled lady who would only perform when her champagne level had reached just about the level of her eyeballs, and then she would sing the bawdiest songs with the most ladylike delivery.

We served full meals and the food was just edible, but not cheap. It would have been cheaper and tastier to eat the money. On New Year's Eve, we obviously had a sellout. I recall with minimal pleasure one of our titled customers, one Lord Burghesh. (I hope I've spelt it absolutely right!) By flashing his title, he succeeded in obtaining a table for himself and a number of friends. As an expression of his gratitude, he made pleasant remarks like: "Only thing wrong with this place, it's full of the Chosen People." This to me, of all people, in passing. But at the end of a rowdy night he left a munificent half-crown tip under his plate, for all his party. He must have felt that this magnanimity made everything all right!

Occasionally, Celia Burnett would take my Celia and me backstage at the Palladium and that was wildly exciting. Once, when Martha Raye came off stage to the number one dressing room, she was bathed in perspiration and whipped off her bra, which in view of her generous dimensions was quite a sight. I certainly found it interesting! I believe Celia B helped her out with her own bra: it could not have been my Celia ... she did not have the attributes. Later, we all walked round to the club from the stagedoor and it was an overwhelming experience to have masses of fans following us and screaming things like: "I've touched her, look, I've touched her!"

Until now, I have refrained from mentioning the most important person of all: Monte Rose, manager of the Stork. He kept performers and customers in line and released Al for his all-important socialising and entertaining. With his dark, wavy hair, Monte was smoothly handsome, despite a slightly chipped front tooth that had almost become a trade mark. He was a very fast, very cultured talker. This was a relic from his own Empire tours, where he ran a supporting act doing rapid-fire commentary for on-stage table tennis performed by professional champions such as Victor Barna and Richard Bergman. Monte and Celia began to make sheep's eyes at each other. Well, he was nearing forty and Celia was late twenties and voila! in a few months they were married. One did that sort of thing in those days: one actually got married! He used to say to me: "Kid, your sister's got twinkling legs." And most of the time they were happy, Celia and Monte. But material success generally eluded them and they had financial ups and downs that made the Blackpool big dipper look like an anthill. They were cataclysmic. Yet they stayed together and loved each other and had two children, Susan and Peter, with whom I am always in touch and now, Celia and Monte are dead, Al Burnett is dead and probably most of the others whom I have mentioned.

Interlude: I am back where all this glittering writing started, on my balcony in Mallorca. We are being visited by Barbara's sister Thelma and her husband Sidney, my friend for more than forty years. The weather is unusually dull and so it is a good day for writing and reminiscing and of course the memories are now becoming closer and sadder. So much has happened...

Away with the miseries! The work at the Stork Rooms had been great, but it meant travelling home to my Dartmouth Park Hill council flat by first tram at six most mornings. Then up for work at our little workshop in Camden Town from 10 a.m. till late afternoon. Sometimes, after the club, we all went for a kipper breakfast in a café in Woodstock Street, off Bond Street. I think it was called the Orchard, and that was great fun. Oh yes, real showbiz lifestyle! But clearly, even at my young age, this pace could not be sustained and events that were occurring elsewhere began to take over my life.

It had all started with my mother obtaining that handsome, large ten shillings per week council flat on Dartmouth Park Hill for Celia and for me when I came home from the Army. The flat's position near Highgate Hill was impressive and the rooms large and bright, but its appointments and decor left everything to be desired. Plain wooden plank floors ... who'd ever heard of carpets? ... white-washed walls and the cheapest of second hand furniture. I still can't work out where Mother got it all from, although of course she had been receiving my open-handed overwhelming dependant's allowance from the Army, so that with some help from Celia, she contrived for us this high style of living. Until then, Celia had resided in a Home for Young Ladies supplied by her then employers, British Home Stores. This was a frequent practice at that time. On leave from the Army, I had soon discovered that it could be a very exciting experience visiting my sister and her lady-friends and colleagues, up there on the so aptly named Primrose Hill.

Not very long after my demob, Mother exploded her own bomb-shell. She was getting married again! While I was still away, she had met this Scottish Jewish gentleman of mature years. Of Polish origin, Barnet Adler had achieved a comfortable standard of living for himself and his family, consisting of two sons by his first marriage and then five, repeat five, daughters by the second, two of whom were as yet unmarried, so my arrival on the scene put an instant twinkle into Barnet's eye.

This twinkle achieved no reciprocity from me. Anyway, Mother had only awaited my return for the wedding preparations to go ahead. We met our stepfather-to-be at the Cumberland Hotel in London and we all got along just fine. Then came the marriage. The wedding feast was given by my beautiful Aunt Henni and her husband Bernhardt at their home in Edgware. It was a lovely party attended by the Dessaus, Rotensteins etc., and Mother was a knockout! We were all truly very happy for her. So, off they went, my newly-wed mother and her new groom, to live more or less happily ever after, in his delightful home at Doonfoot, near Ayr, on the Scottish coast.

With Mother's departure to the frozen North, Celia and I had the flat to ourselves. I certainly would not like to suggest that Celia took any kind of advantage of this new-found freedom, but for me, oh boy! The lovely hat-check girl from the Stork (she had legs as long as the Eiffel Tower) became a welcome visitor and so did Topsy, also living back in London by then. There were certainly thoughts of marriage in her mind, but I resolutely closed mine to any such ideas ... I just wasn't ready.

Chapter 37

M<small>Y LITTLE PECCADILLOES</small> in Germany had included a relationship with a wealthy young German widow from Bielefeld. Her name was Lore. She had her own apartment and actually owned a car, unheard-of wealth in those days. She wanted me to stay on in Germany, but Topsy had remained firmly on the scene and she wanted to get back to the UK. "How happy could I be with either . . ." Lore's idea would have fitted in well with the proposition from the Army that I sign on for a further two years, in return for a commission. The offer was truly tempting, but I was by then very tired of the whole fruitless interrogation and investigation business. It was getting me down, so that by the time Demob Group 56 arrived in July of '47, I was ready to return home. We had a demob party to outdo all demob parties. It was a wild men-only affair at which we all, including the CO, became uproariously, outstandingly drunk. On arrival I had been handed my own personal bottle of Black Label whisky and it was only after I had lovingly demolished a lethal part of it that I heaved myself into my VW and somehow drove back to my billet. In a serious, laborious, concentrated effort to sober myself up, I stepped straight into the cold shower, very properly dressed in uniform, belt, beret and boots. Nothing sloppy about this sergeant!

Meanwhile, Topsy had every right to want to see us both back home in England and to pursue her own plans of marriage. But that really did not suit me and after some months in London she emigrated to Los Angeles. We corresponded a few times but that was that. As for Lore, she had long since faded into near-oblivion. I am sure that she found a replacement for me in very quick time.

The morning after my demob party, heavily burdened by an

almighty headache, I started my homeward journey through Cux-haven and Hull. I have already related the events which followed over the next few months in London. Financially, things had become particularly bleak. With Celia's marriage and the end of C&B Fashions, Uncle Victor urged me to come to Nottingham, so I ended my nightclub career and disposed of our flat. Uncle Victor generously employed me in his much enlarged business, albeit in a lowly position. That brief period of time was also spent in resuming my agreeable social life in Nottingham, with the help of Joe and Manfred. Then my stepfather suggested that I try my luck in Scotland, perhaps in some kind of partnership. I was to stay with him and Mother. As I have already hinted, he may have harboured some thought of wedded bliss between his youngest daughter and myself. For me this was anathema although she was pretty and very friendly. But I liked Scotland a lot and stayed.

After some early disagreements, Barnet and I became fast friends. However, I thought it easier for my mother if I were to move away to Glasgow and duly settled into digs there. It was not my fault that the landlady had two marriageable daughters. The hopeful looks from the mother, particularly on behalf of one of the girls, soon made it expedient to shake the dust of this particular lodging off my feet. I moved in with a wonderful lady called Rosie Lewis. It was by now becoming clear that Glasgow would be my base and I wanted to begin to develop a settled, constructive lifestyle.

About then I was invited to the wedding in London of my cousin Joe. The amazing coincidence was that Joe was marrying a lovely girl called Della Finer whom I had mildly romanced during the War, but with slightly less honourable intentions. So I borrowed the money for the flight to London and, rented dinner suit lovingly packed, joined Mother on my first-ever aeroplane journey. I dare say it was she who had lent me the money for the trip. Yes, I did manage to be air-sick ... but I was helped by the cooling touch of the air

Oath of Allegiance.

I, NORBERT KUTNER

swear by Almighty God that I will be faithful and bear true allegiance to His Majesty, King George the Sixth, His Heirs and Successors, according to law.

(Signature)

Sworn and subscribed this 4th day of June 1947, before me,

(Signature)

Justice of the Peace for

A Commissioner for Oaths.

Name and Address
(in Block Capitals)

T. CRONIN MAJOR R.A.
Y.C.I.C. B.A.O.R.

Unless otherwise indicated hereon, if the Oath of Allegiance is not taken within one calendar month after the date of this Certificate, the Certificate shall not take effect.

Wt 0186 80 bks/2/47 Wt & Sons Ltd 69o/1712—24

hostess' hand. In those days they still did that. It made flying much more interesting. Then came the second miraculous coincidence: another guest of the wedding we were attending was one Ignaz Kliger, a very close friend of my father's from way back in the old Chemnitz days! He was a manufacturer of ladies' dressing gowns and offered me his Scottish agency which I accepted with well-concealed alacrity. It was a very auspicious moment although it was a surprise to me that anyone could stitch together a living in dressing-gowns. The firm was called "Kay Sidney" and it really started a new life for me. I discovered that I could "sell". I acquired a civilised 1938 Austin Ascot motor car on hire-purchase (£180 including the registration No. BGG1).

The rust and the breakdowns had to be generously overlooked. Thus handsomely equipped, I seriously proceeded to enlarge my business and social life. Among the good friends I made in the Community were the brothers David and Maurice Greenberg and a little later Sidney Shear, who at that time was a struggling photographer. He drove a van which made my car look like a luxury limousine. The floorboards were so thin that he could have put his feet through them and pedalled.

By now I had consciously started the daunting process of educating Bob. I had held on to my knowledge of French, Italian and German and my English was fluent. I no longer had to scratch my head over the pronunciation or meaning of "No Thoroughfare for Vehicles". I was no longer confused by such jolly, subtle shadings of meaning and spelling as in bough, how, rough, cough, cuff, cow, sow, sew etc. And above all, no longer did I believe "ze time is ze money" to be the guiding principle that ruled every Englishman's waking hours. Back in 1945, at the height of my storming campaign through Germany, I had been offered British nationality by a grateful Government. Away at last with that embarrassment of a Polish passport. At a very small ceremony I had received my naturalisation papers and henceforth felt that it was incumbent upon me to act and speak like a true Brit! Now "ze time is ze money" belonged to the past, to 1939 and a fifteen-year-old knickerbockered refugee boy who had been booted out of school at fourteen-and-a-half. I may not have chosen to return to school after settling in England, but in time I discovered a great liking for classical literature and did quite a lot of reading in general. I managed to reduce the gap in my education to the sad level that you are having to contend with here and now.

Thus I had made my life in Glasgow. Mother and Barnet were still living in Ayr and even John had succeeded in coming to see us in Scotland. During his London stay, he frequently enjoyed Celia's and Monte's hospitality and Mother and I helped when we could, which in my case was not often, but at least he did enjoy a reasonably good time while in England.

Now I must take a great leap into the future. Since writing this chronicle, John has died at the age of eighty and even now, I am still discovering some of the strange facts about him. He never acknowledged his first son Luca, who of course never knew his father's real name. Nor did the children and wives of his subsequent marriages. They all continued to live under his adopted identity, the identity of a man long dead in Italy. He never even allowed them to meet his brother and sisters and so Luca did not discover until much later that this family existed. John maintained these mysteries about himself until the very end and I am convinced he took some of this history with him to the grave. I have always felt that he lived in fear of something way back in his past. My niece Claudia, daughter of the second marriage, is however a bright young woman. Having herself married, she started trying to unravel the mysteries of her father's life. She somehow managed to trace her brother Luca in Italy and then prised the rest out of me. When finally she heard that I was working on this book, she bullied me into letting her read it. For a long time I resisted because I felt that I should preserve my brother's secrets. But then the book appeared and gradually she had all the pieces of his saga in her hands. Now the families know that they do not carry his birth name. For years he had made up stories about himself and even explained our different surnames by saying that *I* had changed *my* name! this was probably one of the things that made Claudia suspicious. After all, who would voluntarily choose a name like Kutner! Other clues began to appear here and there so she kept digging!

The last time I heard from him he phoned me to Mallorca from his deathbed. He said, "I am very ill, Bob." But even then there were no deathbed confessions and thus ends the story of my brother John, hard guy, egotist, hero.

I had made the acquaintance of a lovely, tall, willowy blonde by the name of Fiona McFarlane. She came from a somewhat elite Scottish background. I suppose for me that was an added attraction. As they said in the old penny-dreadfuls, our friendship ripened. At that time, she was attending a finishing school in London called the Monkey Club in Pont Street, close to Buckingham Palace. On business visits to London, I was occasionally allowed to call.

One day she invited me to escort her to a very elegant party in London's West End. She also invited my cousin Manfred as a blind date for one of her girlfriends. Before calling for them, Manfred and I stopped off for a few drinks, particularly yours truly; so that when we arrived for the girls, I felt pretty much as I had felt at my demob party. With me driving my super magnificent Triumph Razor Edge saloon complete with genuine leather seats, we just managed to reach the festivities. On arrival I was handed a double outsize whisky before crossing the doorstep. That did for me! All down one side of the very large reception area, there was a long, extended trestle table, lavishly covered from beginning to end with delicacies that our post-war minds were only just beginning to get accustomed to. Don't ask me how I slipped, but slip I did! In extending my hand for balance, I grabbed the table which sadly did not prevent me from falling flat on my face, bringing down the entire artistic table arrangement with an almighty crash! Glasses, bottles, plates, cutlery, flowers, food: the lot collapsed, unfortunately with me under it! To conclude this humiliating recital, let me confess that my presence did not appear to have enhanced the party! I did not make my exit to a round of thunderous applause. Nor did my little mishap do anything to improve my relationship with the lovely Fiona. She was supposed to travel back to Glasgow with me the following day, but she easily decided to forego this pleasure and thus ended another beautiful friendship.

Chapter 38

PERSONAL CHRONICLES that start with so many problems are surely entitled to a happy ending. But judge for yourselves. Through Sidney Shear I met my future wife Barbara, sister of his girlfriend Thelma, and I was always made extremely welcome by her very hospitable parents, Mabel and Joe Stone. Other young people were always in and out of the house and in that atmosphere I felt very much at home and that was something I had not experienced for a long time.

Thelma and Sidney became engaged, which was no surprise to anyone. Barbara naturally was asked to be best maid and I was proud to be invited to be Sidney's best man. It was a splendid wedding though Joe Stone chose that occasion to take me aside and give me a gentle little lecture on the very visibly growing bond between Barbara and myself. He felt she was too young for me and that I should bear that very seriously in mind. He never offered any other criticism or restraint. In private with Barbara I must admit that I too was concerned about the age-difference, but she felt adult and mature enough for us to marry. And of course she was, a fact she has demonstrated ever since. Anyway, we were in love and needed no persuasion. On a very romantic night at a dinner dance at Forest Hills in the Highlands, I proposed formally to Babs and was joyfully accepted. She even had the wisdom and maturity to sound a little surprised. This time Joe and Mabel were entirely delighted, with the proviso that we wait a few months before announcing our engagement. I will not tell you about our courtship, for it is nobody else's business, but I still remember Thelma's squeal of delight when we first told her and to this day, I still hear Sidney's frequent complaint

Barbara and I in 1967

that he had exchanged a friend for a brother-in-law. And Joe beamed. Hadn't it all gone nicely by the book?

Barbara and I made our engagement public on her birthday in October 1952. She was all of seventeen years old! We married in June 1953. Barbara was splendid in her dazzling white gown and veil with pearl tiara and, dressed in my rented morning suit and top hat, I did the supporting act, as I have done ever since. A long way from the knickerbocker suit!

Now, forty-some years later, we have together entered the late 1990s. So little time to the millennium and still closely together with our daughter Lesley and son Tony and our two grandsons, Joshua and Daniel ... And Thelma ... And Sidney ... And all our family ... And the ever young indefatigable Mabel.

The rest is another story ...

Postscript

Grandparents Kutner died concentration camp.

Friedman family died concentration camp.

Grandfather Rotenstein died Nottingham September 1943.

Grandmother Betti Rotenstein died Nottingham October 1969.

Uncle Victor Dessau died Nottingham February 1961.

Aunt Gina Dessau died Nottingham April 1980.

Monte Rose died London December 1978.

Celia Rose died London April 1993.

Mother died Glasgow April 1991.

Joe Stone died Glasgow October 1982.

My brother John died Brazil January 1999.

Epilogue

"Luck," said Somerset Maugham, "is a talent." Humbly accepting that philosophy, I, a very ordinary man, must have had talent showered upon me. Just to have been able to spend these last years looking back upon an early life of some adventure and colour and latterly a very modest degree of achievement, surrounded by all my family and friends, I consider very fortunate indeed.

Glasgow, Scotland.